MISSION OF THE *MESSIAH*

*Dedicated in gratitude
to my mother and father,
Judy and Gary Gray.*

MISSION OF THE MESSIAH

On the Gospel of Luke

Tim Gray

EMMAUS ROAD
PUBLISHING
Steubenville, Ohio

Emmaus Road Publishing
1468 Parkview Circle
Steubenville, Ohio 43952

Library of Congress Control Number: 98-074365
ISBN: 0-9663223-1-2
ISBN: 978-0-966322-31-6

On the cover
Rembrandt van Rijn, *Head of Christ*

Cover design and layout by
Beth Hart

Nihil Obstat: Rev. James M. Dunfee, *Censor Librorum*
Imprimatur: ✠ Gilbert I. Sheldon, D.D., D.Min., Bishop of Steubenville
September 14, 1998

CONTENTS

ABBREVIATIONS

The Old Testament
Gen./Genesis
Ex./Exodus
Lev./Leviticus
Num./Numbers
Deut./Deuteronomy
Josh./Joshua
Judg./Judges
Ruth/Ruth
1 Sam./1 Samuel
2 Sam./2 Samuel
1 Kings/1 Kings
2 Kings/2 Kings
1 Chron./1 Chronicles
2 Chron./2 Chronicles
Ezra/Ezra
Neh./Nehemiah
Tob./Tobit
Jud./Judith
Esther/Esther
Job/Job
Ps./Psalms
Prov./Proverbs
Eccles./Ecclesiastes
Song/Song of Solomon
Wis./Wisdom
Sir./Sirach (Ecclesiasticus)
Is./Isaiah
Jer./Jeremiah
Lam./Lamentations
Bar./Baruch
Ezek./Ezekiel
Dan./Daniel
Hos./Hosea

Joel/Joel
Amos/Amos
Obad./Obadiah
Jon./Jonah
Mic./Micah
Nahum/Nahum
Hab./Habakkuk
Zeph./Zephaniah
Hag./Haggai
Zech./Zechariah
Mal./Malachi
1 Mac./1 Maccabees
2 Mac./2 Maccabees

The New Testament
Mt./Matthew
Mk./Mark
Lk./Luke
Jn./John
Acts/Acts of the Apostles
Rom./Romans
1 Cor./1 Corinthians
2 Cor./2 Corinthians
Gal./Galatians
Eph./Ephesians
Phil./Philippians
Col./Colossians
1 Thess./1 Thessalonians
2 Thess./2 Thessalonians
1 Tim./1 Timothy
2 Tim./2 Timothy
Tit./Titus
Philem./Philemon
Heb./Hebrews

Jas./James
1 Pet./1 Peter
2 Pet./2 Peter
1 Jn./1 John
2 Jn./2 John
3 Jn./3 John
Jude/Jude
Rev./Revelation (Apocalypse)

Catechism of the Catholic Church

Throughout the text, the *Catechism of the Catholic Church* will be cited simply as Catechism.

FOREWORD

I remember taking my first step onto Israeli soil like it was yesterday. For years prior to my visit, I had read the Bible, imagining how the cities, mountains, and rivers must have looked. Until my first visit to the Holy Land, I considered myself relatively familiar with the Bible, but I was amazed at how my understanding of the Bible grew once I related the biblical narrative to the stage on which the drama took place. On that first pilgrimage, I daily experienced a surge of excitement every time I recalled a biblical story while standing on the very site on which it occurred.

Now I read the Bible differently. The biblical accounts have a geographic backdrop that not only helps to clarify and bring to life particular passages, but also helps me to relate each passage to the rest of the biblical narrative. I often recall those familiar sites, sounds, and smells of the Holy Land. Yes, I would have to say I left Israel with a sense of owning many of the Bible stories. They were mine to meditate on forever. This is the treasure one finds when the details of a story are seen against the bigger picture.

In the same way that the reader is restricted by not being able to place the biblical narrative geographically, the student of Scripture is also disadvantaged when he does not understand the relationship between the Old and New Testaments. The Church teaches that there is a unity of the divine plan in the two testaments, through what is called *typology*. In other words, the Old Testament prefigures what God accomplished in the fullness of time in the Person of His incarnate Son, Jesus Christ.

The Catechism states it well:

> Christians therefore read the Old Testament in the light of Christ crucified and risen. Such typological reading discloses the inexhaustible content of the Old Testament; but it must not make us forget that the Old Testament retains its own intrinsic value as Revelation reaffirmed by Our Lord Himself. Besides, the New Testament has to be read in the light of the Old. Early Christian catechesis made constant use of the Old Testament. As an old saying put it, the New Testament lies hidden in the Old and the Old Testament is unveiled in the New (no. 129).

This is the genius of Tim Gray's treatment of the Gospel of Luke. He demonstrates how the Old Testament is unveiled in the Gospel, leaving the reader with that surge of excitement that only comes upon the discovery of something great.

When reading through the New Testament, one realizes that he is reading over material that presupposes a knowledge of underlying concepts such as the role of Elijah in the coming of the Messiah, or the relationship between the phrase "proclaim release" and the year of Jubilee. Gray masterfully describes the meaning of key concepts and then weds passages from Luke to their Old Testament backdrop in a way that simply makes the text sing.

For example, when Luke states that John the Baptist would have "the spirit and power of Elijah" (Lk. 1:17), we understand immediately that the evangelist wants the reader to see that there is a relation-ship between the two prophets. But Gray helps us to further understand the depth of Luke's words by drawing our attention to the fact that the last place Elijah goes is to the Jordan River, which is the first place we see John in his public ministry, thus giving the reader a sense of continuity and harmony.

Of particular interest to the reader might be Gray's insights on the Jubilee Year. As he writes,

> At the heart of Jesus' mission, which is signaled by His declaration of a new jubilee year, is the release from the worst form of bondage, the debt of sin. . . . Sin is the central target of Jesus' messianic mission; and the mighty deeds of Jesus are the signs that, through Him, sin is dealt with in a definitive way (p. 43).

Mission of the Messiah will serve as a tremendous catechetical tool in preparation for the Year of Jubilee, as each chapter concludes with a series of questions designed for personal reflection or group discussion. Clergy and laymen alike will find *Mission of the Messiah* filled with practical insights.

There is such a need today for material that distills what could be technically overwhelming truths into understandable morsels for the layman. The book you are holding does just that. I found that I could not put it down, because I knew that just around the corner, in the next chapter, Gray was going to give me another one of those insights that leave you saying, "Yes! Yes! Yes!"

When you finish reading *Mission of the Messiah*, remember to write your name on the inside cover, because others are going to want to know where you found your new insights. Better yet, buy your friends a copy. This is too good to keep to yourself. Enjoy!

Jeffery Cavins
Birmingham, AL

INTRODUCTION

The One Thing Needful

Saint Thérèse of Lisieux loved Scripture. She loved Scripture because her heart was captured by Christ. Among all the books of Scripture, the Gospels most captured Thérèse's attention. She clearly perceived that the Gospels were the heart of Scripture, because they most directly manifested the Sacred Heart of Jesus. Indeed, when the *Catechism of the Catholic Church* teaches that the Gospels are to have pride of place among all Scripture, it quotes Saint Thérèse to exemplify the love of the Gospels that is characteristic of the saints:

> But above all it's the Gospels that occupy my mind when I'm at prayer; my poor soul has so many needs, and yet this is *the one thing needful*. I'm always finding fresh lights there, hidden and enthralling meanings (Catechism, no. 127, emphasis added).

The Gospels were the font from which Thérèse drew her consolation and contemplation of Jesus.

The Church has named Thérèse a doctor of the Church, which means that her teaching is not only sound, but so profound that the Church recommends it to the faithful in every age. Saint Thérèse would have us learn "the one thing needful," the contemplation of Christ through the Gospel. Indeed, Thérèse's spiritual axiom is the fruit of her own contemplation of Christ in Scripture. Yet it is also an echo to one of the stories of Jesus that Luke records in his Gospel.

The story is a familiar one, but one in which the Little Flower discerned a life-changing insight:

> Now as they went on their way, he entered a village; and a woman named Martha received him into her house. And she had a sister called Mary, who sat at the Lord's feet and listened to his teaching. But Martha was distracted with much serving; and she went to him and said, "Lord, do you not care that my sister has left me to serve alone? Tell her then to help me." But the Lord answered her, "Martha, Martha, you are anxious and troubled about many things; *one thing is needful*. Mary has chosen the good portion, which shall not be taken away from her" (Lk. 10:38-42).

Thérèse chose the "good portion" and, by prioritizing the one thing needful in the midst of life's troubles and anxieties, she became a saint. It is easy to identify with Martha—we often feel the weight of work and all the things that need to be done. But the challenge is to put first things first, worship before work: Seek first "his kingdom, and these things shall be yours as well" (Lk. 12:31).

Thérèse, like Martha's sister Mary, understood that the one thing we most need is to contemplate Christ. Just as Mary sat at Jesus' feet to hear His words of wisdom, so too Thérèse sat at the feet of Jesus by reading the holy Gospels. We too must come to Christ through the contemplation of Scripture, drinking deeply from the wellsprings of worship: *the Gospels*.

Saint Jerome, the patron saint of biblical studies, once observed that "[i]gnorance of the Scriptures is ignorance of Christ" (quoted in Catechism, no. 133). Jerome keenly understood why the study and contemplation of Scripture is the one thing needful. To the extent that we do not know the Bible, we likewise do not know our Lord and Savior Jesus Christ.

God gave us Scripture so that we could understand His greatest gift to us, His Son. The gift of the "Word made written" sheds light on the Word made flesh, and likewise the Word made flesh enlightens our reading of Scripture. Scripture is a lamp that illuminates Jesus, and Jesus is a light that illuminates Scripture.

One of the best ways to know Jesus is through Scripture. Indeed, this is the method that Jesus Himself employed in teaching His disciples! At the end of his Gospel, Saint Luke recounts Jesus' encounter with two of His disciples on the road to Emmaus. The story highlights how Jesus explained who He was and the meaning of His messianic mission through Scripture. The story begins with two disciples walking back from Jerusalem to Emmaus, immediately after the tragic Passover at which Jesus was crucified. Along the way, Jesus, now resurrected, joins them as they walk along the road; but they fail to recognize Him.

> [Jesus] said to them, "What is this conversation which you are holding with each other as you walk?" And they stood still, looking sad. Then one of them, named Cleopas, answered him, "Are you the only visitor to Jerusalem who does not know the things that have happened there in these days?" And he said to them, "What things?" And they said to him, "Concerning Jesus of Nazareth, who was a prophet mighty in deed and word before God and all the people, and how our chief priests and rulers deliv-

ered him up to be condemned to death, and crucified him. But we had hoped that he was the one to redeem Israel" (Lk. 24:17-21).

They thought that Jesus' mission to redeem Israel had failed, and so their hope that Jesus was the Messiah died on the Cross. But unbeknownst to them, He was risen from the dead and speaking to them! Jesus exclaims:

> "O foolish men, and slow of heart to believe all that the prophets have spoken! Was it not necessary that the Christ should suffer these things and enter into his glory?" And beginning with Moses and all the prophets, he interpreted to them in all the scriptures the things concerning himself (Lk. 24:25-27).

In order to teach them about the significance of His death and Resurrection and the nature of His messianic mission, Jesus gave the disciples a Bible study on the road to Emmaus. The two disciples would never forget that day's walk to Emmaus: "Did not our hearts burn within us while he talked to us on the road, while he opened to us the scriptures?" (Lk. 24:32).

Once, when I was giving a talk on this scene in Luke, an older gentlemen in the audience leaned forward, pointed to his tape recorder, and sighed, "Wouldn't it have been great to have Jesus' conversation on the road to Emmaus recorded?" We may not have a tape recording of Jesus' explanation of Scripture given on the way to Emmaus, but we do have a written record of that conversation. Where? In Luke's Gospel. Remember, Saint Luke begins his Gospel by stating that he is recording what eyewitnesses have seen and heard, and surely among those witnesses would have been the disciples from the road to Emmaus. If we read Luke's Gospel carefully, we shall hear the echoes to the Old Testament, and we shall see how Jesus fulfills the whole story of Scripture.

The goal of this study of Luke is to give a taste of that Bible study Jesus gave on the road to Emmaus. As we study God's holy Word, our hearts too will burn with the fire of God's love (cf. Lk. 12:49), just as the disciples experienced God's love on the dusty road to Emmaus. If we read the Gospel with the prayer and contemplation that Saint Thérèse did, we too shall find "fresh lights there, hidden and enthralling meanings."

1

THE BAPTISM AND ANOINTING OF JESUS
—LUKE 3—

A Voice in the Wilderness

In order to be baptized by John the Baptist, the people of Jerusalem had to take a long, hot hike through the wilderness. Wouldn't it have made more sense for the prophet to preach in Jerusalem? For that matter, wouldn't the Temple in Jerusalem have been a better place for the ritual washing of repentance? Wandering out to the wilderness, some may have wondered why John made the barren, rocky terrain his base of operations, and the Jordan River the place of his baptizing. So why did this holy man and prophet call Jerusalem to journey out to the Jordan and wander in the wilderness?

The explanation may be found in the Old Testament. Luke illustrates the prophetic purpose of John's preaching in the wilderness by quoting from Isaiah. "The voice of one crying in the wilderness: Prepare the way of the Lord, make his paths straight" (Lk. 3:4). Isaiah had foretold that the wilderness would be the place of origin for Israel's new exodus, which would be announced by a voice crying out. This announcement comes at the beginning of the second half of Isaiah. Why is this important?

The context is the key, for Isaiah has two very distinct parts, so much so that some scholars believe that there must have been at least two different authors of Isaiah. The first part of Isaiah (1-39), which could be called the Book of Woes, is about the bad news that Israel will end up exiled for her sins. The second half of Isaiah (40-66) is known as the Book of Consolation, because of the soothing words it imparts in contrast to the ominous and heart-wrenching warning of the first half. The Book of Consolation gave hope to the Jewish exiles that, despite their travails, one day Yahweh would pardon their sins and liberate them from their captivity.

This is what the Jews of John the Baptist's day longed for—the fulfillment of the second half of Isaiah. The first half of Isaiah had already come true. The Jews were conquered by the Babylonians, who deported them out of the Holy Land. Even though many of the Jews had returned to the Promised Land by Jesus' day, they still lived in virtual exile.[1] Although the Babylonians did not rule them, the Romans did. All the Jews of John's day knew that the first half of Isaiah had tragically taken place, so they were all patiently waiting for the good news of the second half to unfold. This, according to Luke, is exactly what is happening with John's mission in the wilderness. By citing the opening verses of Isaiah 40, Luke is claiming that John the Baptist marks the beginning of the good news. The Lord of History had finally opened up the Book of Consolation, the book that told the story of Israel's new exodus, of her return from exile. Now the fullness of prophetic time had come.

---

[1] While many Jews had returned from Babylon by Jesus' day, the exile had by no means ended. Nehemiah, who was one of the leaders of the Jews who returned from Babylon to Jerusalem, recognized that the remnant of Israel were in a paradoxical situation: the exiles had returned, but the exilic condition of captivity continued. As Nehemiah declared after returning to Jerusalem from Babylon:

> Behold, we are slaves this day; in the land that thou gavest to our fathers to enjoy its fruit and its good gifts, behold, we are slaves. And its rich yield goes to the kings whom thou hast

Why go out to the wilderness? Because according to Isaiah the wilderness was to be the stage where the new exodus would spring up. And now that Isaiah's prophetic voice had taken shape in John the Baptist, it became clear that the time had come for Israel to follow in the sandals of her forbears and make an exodus through the wilderness and across the Jordan. John stirred up more than the waters of the Jordan with his baptizing: He had stirred up the people's hope of a new exodus—this time not from Pharoah, or even Caesar, but from Satan.

Why Wash in the Jordan?

Why did John make Israel wash in the muddy waters of the Jordan? Why is it that this new story starts with Jews jumping into the Jordan in order to be baptized?

John was a prophet, and prophets were known for performing symbolic actions with rich, prophetic meanings. For example, the prophet Jeremiah smashed a pot to symbolize the destruction of the Temple, Hosea took a prostitute as a wife to signify how Israel was an unfaithful bride to Yahweh, and Ezekiel shaved with a sword, not for a closer shave, but to signify the impending invasion of Jerusalem.

---

set over us because of our sins; they have power also over our bodies and over our cattle at their pleasure, and we are in great distress (Neh. 9:36-37).

N.T. Wright, one of the most brilliant scholars on the historical Jesus today (and the most articulate voice against the so-called "Jesus Seminar"), has developed the motifs of exile and exodus in his outstanding historical study on Jesus, *Jesus and the Victory of God* (Minneapolis: Fortress Press, 1996). For a less academic and more popular work, see Wright's *The Original Jesus* (Grand Rapids, MI: Berdmans, 1996).

Prophets performed provocative acts, acts that were aimed at making a mark in the memory and bringing about a change of heart in their audience. John's directing the people of Jerusalem and Judah into the Jordan was an action pregnant with meaning.

The Jordan was a religious and national symbol for the Jews. At the climax of the first exodus, when Israel escaped from Egypt, Joshua led Israel through the Jordan and into the Promised Land. Crossing the Jordan long ago marked Israel's release from Egyptian captivity and the beginning of Israel's possession of the Promised Land. Now John was calling Israel to come back to the Jordan and reenter the Promised Land. Like their ancestors before them, Israel was to go out to the wilderness and then reenter into the Promised Land. John was offering Israel a fresh start, a new beginning. The crowds grew in anticipation and excitement, for it looked like John was beginning the new exodus, the fulfillment of the prophetic promises made by Isaiah.

Many wondered whether John might be the Messiah, the one to lead Israel through a new exodus and redemption. John, however, was not the new Joshua. He made it clear that he was simply preparing the way, saying,

> I baptize you with water; but he who is mightier than I is coming, the thong of whose sandals I am not worthy to untie; he will baptize you with the Holy Spirit and with fire (Lk. 3:16).

The mark of the true Messiah would be the Holy Spirit, and John announced that He was coming soon.

If John is no Joshua, he does have other sandals

to fill. Luke gives his reader an important clue that John is the prophetic protégé of the prophet Elijah. When the angel Gabriel announced to John's father, Zechariah, that he would have a son who would do great things for God, he said that John would have "the spirit and power of Elijah" (Lk. 1:17).

What is so significant about John's being a new Elijah? It just so happens that the final words of Malachi, the last prophet sent to Israel, predict that Elijah will return before the Messiah comes (cf. Mal. 4:5). If one saw John as a type of Elijah, then clearly the time for the Messiah was at hand. It is worth noting that the last place Elijah goes to is the Jordan River. At the Jordan, as the heavens open to take Elijah up in a chariot of fire, he passes on a double portion of his share of the Spirit of God to his successor, Elisha. If John is playing the role of Elijah, the expectation mounts that one is soon coming who will take the reigns from John and possess a greater share of the power of the Spirit. And there is no better place to pass the baton to John's successor than at the Jordan.

Jesus at the Jordan

John summoned all of Israel to come out to the Jordan for baptism. Along with the rest of Israel, Jesus also came to the Jordan in the midst of the Judean wilderness. "Jesus went to be baptized, then, not for private reasons, but as a man with a public calling."[2] He came not as a sinner in need of repentance, but as an Israelite faithful to the prophetic summons.

---

[2] G.B. Caird, *Saint Luke: The Pelican New Testament Commentaries* (New York: Penguin Books, 1963), 77.

Jesus did not need the baptism that John offered, but He submitted in order to take on the role of the suffering servant, the one whom Isaiah prophesied would be innocent and yet "numbered with the transgressors" (Is. 53:12), in order to "bear their iniquities" (Is. 53:11).

Jesus' humble act of accepting baptism drew an immediate response from heaven:

> Now when all the people were baptized, and when Jesus also had been baptized and was praying, the heaven was opened, and *the Holy Spirit descended upon him* in bodily form, as a dove, and a voice came from heaven, "Thou art my beloved Son; with thee I am well pleased" (Lk. 3:21-22).

The Father's words to His beloved Son, Jesus, echo the ancient words spoken by God to the suffering servant in Isaiah in what is known as the first servant song (Is. 42:1-9), at the beginning of the servant's mission:

> Behold my servant, whom I uphold, my chosen, in whom my soul delights; *I have put my Spirit upon him*, he will bring forth justice to the nations (Is. 42:1).

As John noted, the Spirit identifies the Messiah, the servant of the Lord. With the outpouring of the Spirit, Jesus plays Elisha to John's Elijah.

The descent of the Holy Spirit upon Jesus is a turning point in Israel's story, a turning as dramatic as moving from Isaiah's Book of Woes to his Book of Consolation. Just as at the Jordan the torch was passed from Elijah to Elisha, so it is with John and

Jesus. The Holy Spirit comes upon Jesus and anoints Him in the Jordan River.

Yet how can we be sure that Jesus was anointed by the Spirit when the word "anoint" is not found in the baptismal account? The answer comes in the very next chapter of Luke, when Jesus takes the scroll of Isaiah and reads the words of the servant of Isaiah as His own, declaring, "The Spirit of the Lord God is upon me, because *the LORD has anointed me*" (Is. 61:1; cf. Lk. 4:18). Jesus understands that at His baptism the Father anointed Him with the Holy Spirit. In the sequel to his Gospel, the Acts of the Apostles, Luke records how Peter referred to Jesus' baptism as the time when "God anointed Jesus of Nazareth with the Holy Spirit and with power" (Acts 10:38).

With the anointing of the Spirit, Jesus can now be called the Messiah, for in Hebrew "Messiah" literally means "anointed one." Jesus is called the Christ, the Greek word for Messiah, because He was anointed in the power of the Holy Spirit at His baptism in the Jordan. Therefore, "Christ" is not originally a name, but a title. From the moment that Jesus emerges from the waters of the Jordan, He is the Christ, the Messiah. Not without reason is He named Jesus, which is the Greek for Joshua, which itself is Hebrew for "Yahweh saves." The new Joshua has come to lead Israel through the Jordan and to the new Promised Land.

The Royal Meaning of Messiah

The Messiah was the one whom the prophets foretold would redeem Israel and bring about the new exodus. It was known that the Messiah would be a king, because "the Lord's anointed" (Messiah) was a title for the king of Israel. After the prophet Samuel anointed Saul as king of Israel (cf. 1 Sam. 10:1), he told him that one of the signs that the Lord had truly anointed Saul king over Israel was that "the spirit of the LORD will come mightily upon you" (1 Sam. 10:6). This is the same sign that marks Jesus as the Messiah, for the Spirit comes upon Him at His baptism, and Jesus, "full of the Holy Spirit, returned from the Jordan, and was led by the Spirit" (Lk. 4:1). "And Jesus returned in the power of the Spirit into Galilee" (Lk. 4:14). Jesus is the Christ, because the Spirit of the Lord is upon Him.

Immediately after Jesus' baptism and anointing in the Spirit, Luke gives us Jesus' genealogy (cf. Lk. 3:23-28). One of the key aspects of the genealogy is that it proves that Jesus is of the royal line of David. Why give the genealogy at this point in the story, and not earlier during the infancy narrative? Luke places the genealogy here to highlight Jesus' royal status as an heir of David. He can truly be the Messiah, the king of Israel. And by juxtaposing the baptismal scene with the genealogy, Luke can underscore the parallel between Jesus and David, who was anointed in the power of the Spirit when he became king:

> Then Samuel took the horn of oil, and anointed him in the midst of his brothers; and the Spirit of the LORD came mightily upon David from that day forward (1 Sam. 16:13).

Jesus is the son of David (cf. Lk. 3:31), the anointed heir and therefore the Messiah, the king of Israel. Not only that, but by tracing Jesus' genealogy all the way back to Adam, Luke implies that Jesus' reign will extend not only over the family of Abraham, but over all humanity. All of Adam's family will be redeemed through the mission of the Messiah. Isaiah's good news has come in the Person of Jesus, and through His ministry consolation and comfort will be given to all who heed His voice.

* * *

Questions for Reflection
or Group Discussion

1. (a) Have you ever picked up a book, or started watching a movie, in the middle or towards the end, and had difficulty understanding the plot? **(b)** How is that comparable to reading the Gospels without any knowledge of the Old Testament? **(c)** What did you learn about the baptism of Jesus, from the light of the Old Testament, that you did not know before?

_____

_____

_____

2. (a) George Frideric Handel began his musical masterpiece *Messiah* (1742), which tells the story of Jesus from a wide selection of Scripture passages, with the first five verses of Isaiah's fortieth chapter. Given what you have learned about Isaiah, why do you think Handel chose to begin his musical story of the Messiah with those particular verses? **(b)** According to Isaiah 40:1-9, what exactly is the voice in the wilderness supposed to cry out? **(c)** Why do you think Isaiah began with the bad news before announcing the good news?

_____

_____

_____

3. (a) Prophets were known for performing symbolic actions. Can you think of any examples of symbolic actions made in the Old Testament? **(b)** Can you think of any actions, from your cultural and national history, that are remembered as being symbolic (for example, dumping tea into Boston Harbor)? **(c)** What are some of the actions that Jesus performed that might have been symbolic in the manner of the prophets? For example, what would Jesus' baptism have symbolized? (see Catechism, no. 537).

_____

_____

_____

_____

4. (a) If Jesus is called "Christ" because He is anointed by the Holy Spirit, why do you think we are called Christians? **(b)** What difference does it make for Christian identity that we are not just followers of Christ, but anointed in the Spirit like Jesus (that is, that we are "anointed ones")? **(c)** How should the fact that we are anointed with the Spirit affect the way we think and behave? **(d)** Did you know that we are anointed with the Spirit at Baptism, and that the

Sacrament of Confirmation is the confirming of that anointing? (see Catechism, no. 1285).

_____

_____

_____

_____

_____

_____

2

LUKE'S VISION OF JESUS' JUBILEE YEAR
—LUKE 4—

Setting the Stage for the Jubilee

Of all the Gospel writers, Luke alone highlights how Jesus launched His ministry from His hometown of Nazareth. The setting for Jesus' opening proclamation is the synagogue of Nazareth, the very place where He learned the Torah. Jesus unrolls the scroll that holds the prophetic words of Isaiah and reads:

> The Spirit of the Lord is upon me, because he has anointed me to preach good news to the poor; He has sent me to proclaim release to the captives, and recovering of sight to the blind, to set at liberty those who are oppressed, to proclaim the acceptable year of the Lord (Lk. 4:18-19; cf. Is. 61:1-2).

In an astonishingly bold move, Jesus makes the words of Isaiah His own: "Today, this scripture has been fulfilled in your hearing" (Lk. 4:21). Reading from Isaiah's script, Jesus "proclaim[s] release to the captives." To understand the significance of Isaiah's prophecy and Jesus' adoption of it, it is essential to know the rich biblical tradition that the phrase "proclaim release" evokes. This phrase functioned in the Old Testament as a technical idiom for announcing the jubilee year (cf. Lev. 25:10; Deut. 15:2). By claiming that Isaiah's prophecy has been fulfilled, Jesus declares that the springtime of Israel's restoration and renewal—the jubilee year—has arrived: "the acceptable year of the Lord."

The Origins of the Year of Jubilee

In order to better understand Jesus' declaration of a jubilee, we need to see the events of Nazareth against the backdrop of the ancient, year-long festival called the *jubilee*. The Torah, the law of Moses contained in the Bible's first five books, describes the jubilee and its legislation (cf. Lev. 25; Deut. 15). For Israel, the seventh day of the week, the sabbath, was the sign of the covenant God made with her at the time of her Exodus from Egypt. In addition, every seventh year was a sabbath year (from which we get the term "sabbatical"), a yearlong sign of the covenant. After a series of seven sabbath years (for a total of 49 years), the next year, the fiftieth, was to be a year-long festival of joy (jubilation) and celebration (Lev. 25:10). The fiftieth year was the year of jubilee. The jubilee year was the sabbath of sabbaths of sabbaths, the covenant sign par excellence.

Moses gave the people special social legislation that was to be enacted during the jubilee year. These social teachings could be summarized as three precepts: all debts were to be canceled, all slaves freed, and all patrimonial land (inheritance) returned to the family who originally owned the land. How would you like to have all your debts canceled? That's right—all of them, including college loans, credit card balances, car loans, and even your entire mortgage! Each jubilee year, everyone's debts were automatically canceled, no matter the size (Deut. 15:2). There's a cause for celebration!

During the jubilee year, the slaves were set free and given permanent liberty (Lev. 25:10, 39-41). In addition, for those slaves and any other Israelites who had lost the land of their family inheritance, their family land was returned, regardless of any previous sale (Lev. 25:28). Throughout the Old Testament's recording of the jubilee legislation, there is one word that is continually repeated: "release" (Heb. *deror*, Gk. *aphesis*). The slaves were "released," the debts were "released," and the land was "released." Quite simply, the jubilee is the year of "release."

The Jubilee and the Story of Israel

What was the purpose of the jubilee and its social legislation of release? Why release slaves? "You shall remember that you were a slave in the land of Egypt, and the LORD your God redeemed you; therefore I command you this [release of slaves] today" (Deut. 15:15). Why release the land back to families? "I am the LORD your God, who brought you forth out of the land of Egypt to give you the land of Canaan, and to be your God" (Lev. 25:38). Through the Exodus, Yahweh released Israel from slavery in order to give them the Promised Land, the inheritance promised to their ancestor Abraham. Therefore, the social teaching of the jubilee made the festival year not simply a remembrance of the Exodus, but a reenactment of it. The jubilee was to be an internal exodus for Israel. Just as Yahweh liberated Israel from slavery and enriched them in their poverty, so too Israel was to do the same for the poor and needy in her midst. The jubilee celebrates the Exodus by reliving it.

Unfortunately, Israel failed to enact the jubilee liturgy and legislation. This failure, according to the prophet Jeremiah, was the straw that broke the camel's back. Jeremiah describes how the last king to rule Jerusalem, before the Babylonians destroyed the city, tried to enact the jubilee legislation, but the leaders of Jerusalem failed to be faithful to the jubilee. In a last-ditch effort for moral reform, Zedekiah made a "proclamation of liberty" (Jer. 34:8; in Hebrew *kara deror*, with *deror* rendered in the Greek translation by the word *aphesis*, release), which is a technical phrase for declaring a jubilee year and its special social legislation. The wealthy man was then supposed to "set free his Hebrew slaves, male and female, so that no one should enslave a Jew, his brother" (Jer. 34:9). Initially the leaders of Jerusalem swore a covenant oath to enact the jubilee release, "[b]ut afterward they turned around and took back the male and female slaves they had set free" (Jer. 34:11). Then God, through Jeremiah, reminded them that God brought their fathers out of the land of Egypt, out of the house of bondage (cf. Jer. 34:13). They followed neither God's example nor His law. God then announced that, because they have refused to grant release to the poor and needy, He would declare a retributive release:

> You have not obeyed me by proclaiming liberty, every one to his brother and to his neighbor; behold, I proclaim to you liberty to the sword, to pestilence, and to famine, says the LORD (Jer. 34:17).

Finally, they are told that they would go into captivity, since they held captive their own kinsmen (Jer. 34:20). God thus sent Israel into exile so that she could learn the lesson of the exodus once again, through the bitter experience of captivity.

By refusing to imitate God's mercy by freeing

slaves, canceling debts, and taking care of the poor, Israel refused to live by the divine lessons of the Exodus. Because they bound their own kinsmen with debts and chains, Israel, herself, was bound in chains and taken to Babylon.[1] By ignoring the Lord of the Exodus, Israel ended up in exile.

God, however, did not abandon His people. To those in exile, Isaiah promised that there would be a new exodus. God would once again liberate His people and set them free. This liberation would take the shape of the jubilee year. According to Isaiah, the servant of the Lord would be anointed in order to proclaim the year of God's favor, the jubilee year. What better symbol of liberation could Isaiah use for those in captivity than the jubilee, which signified Israel's liberation from Egypt? Now, however, the new slaves to be released were those in exile, the debts to be canceled were Israel's sins, and the land to be restored was Jerusalem and the entire Promised Land.

The Jews anxiously awaited this promised jubilee down to the time of Jesus. One of the ancient Jewish scrolls found in the caves overlooking the Dead Sea is a scroll entitled "The Book of Jubilees." The book recounts the entire history of Israel based on the structure of 50 jubilee years. It is an excellent example of how seriously some Jews took the jubilee.

The group of Jews who authored the Dead Sea Scrolls were known as the Essenes. Many of the Essenes moved out to the wilderness of Judea in order to prepare for the coming of the Messiah, since

---

[1] The prophets in general warn Israel that her lack of charity, particularly in taking care of the most vulnerable, is a primary cause of the exile (cf. Amos 2:6, *et seq.*).

Isaiah foretold that the restoration would begin in the wilderness. Besides the Book of Jubilees, they had another writing which claimed that when the Messiah came He would announce a great jubilee year "to free them from [the debt] of all their iniquities."[2] The Essenes held this belief largely from their reading of Isaiah chapters 58-61. In fact, they believed that the coming of the Messiah and His announcement of the jubilee are the subject of the good news proclaimed in Is. 52:7: "How beautiful upon the mountains are the feet of him who brings good tidings . . . who says to Zion, 'Your God reigns.'" The Essenes illustrate that the Jews of Jesus' day lived in anticipation of Isaiah's prediction and promise concerning the jubilee. The captives pined for the good news that the day of the Lord's jubilee had finally come.

Great Expectations

The Jews who crowded into the synagogue at Nazareth lived in hopeful expectation of the end of their exile and the restoration promised by Isaiah and the prophets. Although many of the exiles had returned to the land by Jesus' day, the pangs of exile still remained. The Romans held Israel captive in their own land. Jesus could not have had a more receptive audience for His jubilee message. Indeed, His words were heard with the wonder of one who, while serving a life sentence in prison, is suddenly informed of his imminent pardon. Yet, within the

---

[2] 11QMelchizedek, trans. by Florentino Garcia Martinez in *The Dead Sea Scrolls Translated: The Qumran Texts in English* (Grand Rapids, MI: Eerdmans Publishing Co., 2nd ed. 1994), 140.

span of several short verses, the wonder turns into wrath, the praise into persecution (cf. Lk. 4:22-30).

What is the reason for this sudden rejection of Jesus? The answer is found in the second part of His jubilee homily. After reading the prophetic passage of Isaiah and declaring its fulfillment, Jesus suggests that the poor who are to be liberated will be like the widow and leper of Elijah and Elisha's day (cf. Lk. 4:25-27). The scandal for Jesus' audience was not that the jubilee liberation would reach out to widows and lepers, but rather that Jesus was making the radical claim that among the widows and lepers experiencing the jubilee would be Gentiles. Many Jews of the time believed that the longed-for jubilee would bring about the vindication of Israel, and would certainly include God's avenging judgment upon Israel's enemies.

It is worth noting that in Jesus' reading of Isaiah He omitted the phrase "the day of vengeance of our God" (Is. 61:2b) and replaced it with "to set at *liberty* (literally in the Greek, "to release") those who are oppressed" (Is. 58:6). Jesus here employs the rabbinic practice of combining two separate passages that share a common word (known as *Gezerah shawah*). Here the word is "release." Jesus' combination of Old Testament passages accentuates the theme of release, but His extension of release to Gentiles, along with His passing over of divine retribution, flies in the face of current Jewish expectation, which longed for vengeance as much as restoration—for any true exodus must include the destruction of Pharaoh's army.

Who Is the Real Enemy?

How could there be any liberation, if there is no enemy to be liberated from? In order to liberate someone from captivity, one must surely fight against those who are holding the captives. How then, and why, does Jesus make the claim that the Gentiles are not the enemy, but rather fellow recipients with the Jews of the jubilee liberation? Is Jesus overlooking the problem of Roman injustice and domination of Israel? No. Jesus' point to Israel is not that things are not as bad as they think, but rather that they are far worse. The Jews have not seen the depth of their plight. Israel's bondage is far stronger than iron chains or Roman soldiers; it consists of a much stronger slavery to sin. Far stronger than the rule of the Romans is the dominion of the devil. Their captivity is not simply a captivity that keeps them from possessing their homeland, but a captivity of the heart, which keeps them from possessing Yahweh Himself.

Thus the "release" that Jesus proclaims and enacts is a release not from soldiers, but from Satan. The Gentiles and the Jews share this common enemy, and both will need the liberation and redemption that Jesus seeks to bring. The release Jesus proclaims and is bringing about cuts far deeper than the old jubilee legislation ever could. The slaves to be freed are those enslaved to sin. The debts to be canceled are the sins of both Jews and Gentiles.[3] The inheri-

---

[3] It would be wrong-headed to spiritualize the debts as only referring to sins, thereby concluding that truly living out the jubilee has nothing to do with releasing people from material debt. Such a reading would fail to discern the spirit of the law, as well as the Holy Spirit, who admonishes us throughout Scripture to take care of the poor. This would not

tance (land) to be restored is not Palestine, but Eden, the original patrimony of Adam and his children. The land to which the new Joshua (Gk. Jesus) will lead His people is the Promised Land of heaven.[4] Jesus puts new wine into the old wineskins of the jubilee.

The Gospel

After preaching in Nazareth, Jesus arrives in Capernaum to preach and teach in the synagogue (Lk. 4:31). When Jesus is ready to leave, the people of Capernaum press Him to stay, but He refuses, saying, "I must preach the good news of the kingdom of God to the other cities also; for I was sent for this purpose" (Lk. 4:43). Pope John Paul II comments on this passage in his 1990 encyclical *Mission of the Redeemer* (no. 13):

> The proclamation and establishment of God's kingdom are the purpose of His mission: "I was sent for this purpose" (Lk. 4:43). But that is not all. Jesus Himself is the "Good News," as He declares at the very beginning of His mission in the synagogue at Nazareth, when He applies to Himself the words of Isaiah about the Anointed One sent by the Spirit of the Lord (cf. Lk. 4:14-21). Since the "Good News" is Christ, there is an identity between the message and the messenger, between saying, doing, and being.

---

only be Saint Francis of Assisi's view, but Pope John Paul II also makes this point in *Tertio Millennio Adveniente*, in which he proclaims a jubilee for the year 2000: "Thus, in the spirit of the Book of Leviticus (25:8-12), Christians will have to raise their voice on behalf of all the poor of the world, proposing the jubilee as an appropriate time to give thought, among other things, to reducing substantially, if not canceling outright, the international debt which seriously threatens the future of many nations" (no. 51).

[4] In Is. 58:10-12, God promises that if the jubilee is truly practiced and the poor are taken care of, then the Lord will bless the land such that it will be like a new Eden.

The prophet Isaiah had foretold that the Messiah would signal the restoration of the kingdom with the announcement of the jubilee. After being anointed in the Jordan, Jesus comes to Nazareth, announces the jubilee, and then goes about Galilee proclaiming the kingdom of God. For those who have ears to hear (cf. Lk. 8:8), the Scriptures are finding their fulfillment in Jesus' words and deeds.

A key characteristic of the Lord's anointed servant, according to Isaiah, is the servant's preaching of the "good news" (Is. 61:1). The term *euangelizasthai* ("to preach good news") is the verb form of the Greek noun *euangelion*, which means "good news," or simply "gospel." In Scripture, Isaiah is the first to employ the concept of good news or gospel. We might think that the term "gospel" was coined by the evangelists to describe the story of Jesus' life, but the term goes all the way back to the eighth century B.C. Isaiah employed the term to describe the proclamation that was to be made to the defeated and disenfranchised Israelites, the proclamation that their God would return to Jerusalem and reign, thereby reestablishing the kingdom:

> How beautiful upon the mountains are the feet of him who brings good tidings [*euangelion*], who publishes peace, who brings good tidings [*euangelion*] of good, who publishes salvation, who says to Zion, "Your God reigns." Hark, your watchmen lift up their voice, together they sing for joy; for eye to eye they see the return of the LORD to Zion (Is. 52:7-8).

The joyful event of Israel's promised return from exile, which is the new exodus Isaiah describes in his Book of Consolation (Is. 40-66), is the content of the "good news." When we hear then that the servant of the Lord is the one who will announce the "good news," we cannot see this term as implying any generic good news, but rather we must view the "good news" through the eyes of Isaiah. It is the good news of Israel's long-awaited release and exodus.

In the first century, there was another usage of the term "good news" (*euangelion*) besides the Jewish one. In the Greco-Roman world, *euangelion* was a technical term that declared an epic event, which could range from the birth of an emperor to a smashing military victory. For example, an ancient Roman calendar inscription from about 9 B.C. declared the following concerning the emperor Augustus: "The birthday of the god was for the world the beginning of *joyful tidings* [i.e., good news] which have been proclaimed on his account."[5] Augustus was considered a savior because he brought the end of a long period of civil war.

For the Romans, the emperor Augustus is the subject of joyful tidings as the political "savior" of Rome, but Luke has other ideas. Although a Gentile, Luke unhesitantly subverts the Roman idea that Caesar is the source of salvation and good news. Luke's Gospel declares that the good news began in a remote region of the Roman Empire, in the backwater town of Bethlehem. Luke underscores how Jesus' birth took place at the time of Augustus' reign (Lk. 2:1) to suggest who the *real* source of good news is for the

---

[5] William Lane, *The Gospel of Mark* (Grand Rapids, MI: Eerdmans Publishing Company, 1974), 43.

world. Rather than the empty *pax romana*, the angels herald the good news of the birth of Him who is the real Prince of Peace, Jesus (cf. Is. 9:6; Lk. 2:10-14).

It is easy to forget how countercultural Luke's Gospel was in the Roman world. Many who read Luke and believed that Jesus—and not Caesar—was Savior and Lord, were hunted down and martyred. The Romans burned any copy of the Gospels they could find. With the powerful connotations of *euangelion*, both to Jews and Romans, it is little wonder then that Jesus' proclamation of the good news sparked excitement and controversy.

With a firm understanding of Isaiah's prediction concerning the Lord's anointed, the proclamation of the jubilee, and the announcement of the gospel, or good news, we have the key backdrop from which to see Jesus and His messianic mission. As we shall see in the following chapters, the jubilee provides a powerful lens through which Jesus' words and deeds will come into sharper focus. Thus, as we contemplate Jesus through the lens of the jubilee, we shall see why Pope John Paul II declares that "the words and deeds of Jesus thus represent the fulfillment of the whole tradition of jubilees in the Old Testament."[6]

* * *

---

[6] Pope John Paul II, *Tertio Millennio Adveniente*, no. 12.

Questions for Reflection
or Group Discussion

1. **(a)** What is the historical event behind the jubilee liturgy and laws? **(b)** Why do you think God gave Israel precepts that commanded the release of slaves, debts, and inheritance (patrimonial land) every fifty years? **(c)** How does the call for the release of slaves, debts, and inheritance (land) challenge Israel to reenact the exodus by imitating Yahweh? **(d)** Do you think there is a link today between debt and bondage or slavery, as there was in ancient times? **(e)** What is the biblical view of debt?

_____

_____

_____

_____

2. **(a)** Jesus considers the worst form of bondage to be enslavement to sin. How does sin enslave us? **(b)** In what ways would following Jesus liberate us from the bondage to sin?

_____

_____

_____

3. **(a)** The people in Nazareth rejected Jesus' message because it called for the forgiveness and benefit of their enemies. It was as hard for the people of Palestine to forgive Romans as it would be for people to forgive each other today in such places as Kosovo, Rwanda, Northern Ireland, or even Palestine. Given world history and human nature, do you think it's surprising that His call for forgiveness is the most controversial aspect of His mission? **(b)** How does the failure to forgive create division not only among ethnic groups and nations, but within our own families and communities?

_____

_____

_____

_____

4. (a) What is the good news that Isaiah prophesies to the people in exile? **(b)** What is the good news that Jesus came to announce, and how does it relate to Isaiah? **(c)** In what way does Jesus fulfill both the Jewish and Gentile understanding of "good news"? **(d)** In what ways is the message of Jesus still good news for the world today? **(e)** How can we share the good news of Jesus with the people we know or meet in our everyday lives? **(f)** Is the Gospel still counter-cultural in our day as it was in Luke's?

_____

_____

_____

_____

_____

_____

3

SIGNS OF THE KINGDOM OF GOD
—LUKE 5, 7-8—

At the heart of the jubilee is the gratuitous release from debt and its bondage. At the heart of Jesus' mission, which is signaled by His declaration of a new jubilee year, is the release from the worst form of bondage, the debt of sin. Jesus' mission of releasing people from the bonds of sin is intertwined with His healing ministry, where He grants release to those in bondage to illness and disease. Indeed, Jesus' mighty healings manifest the interior healing that comes from the forgiveness of sins. Sin is the central target of Jesus' messianic mission; and the mighty deeds of Jesus are the signs that, through Him, sin is dealt with in a definitive way.

Forgiveness of Sins

Jesus' teaching and ministry enkindled some serious criticism, primarily from the Pharisees. Jesus responded to His critics by showing the absurdity of their charges. On the one hand, Jesus' critics had accused John the Baptist of being crazy and possessed by a demon because he ate no bread and drank no wine (Lk. 7:33). On the other hand, since Jesus ate bread and drank wine, they accused Him of being "a glutton and a drunkard, a friend of tax collectors and sinners" (Lk. 7:34).

Jesus unveils the conflicting and ridiculous nature of the charges. His critics must have felt the sting of Jesus' rebuke, for Simon, one of the Pharisees, immediately invites Him to dinner. Is the invitation disingenuous or sincere? Is it simply a knee-jerk reaction, an attempt to put on a good face for the public?

Whatever the motives for the invitation, the irony between the charges and the dinner invitation comes into sharper focus with the arrival of a surprise guest. As soon as Jesus is seated at Simon's table,

> a woman of the city, who was a sinner . . . brought an alabaster flask of ointment, and standing behind him at his feet, weeping, she began to wet his feet with her tears, and wiped them with the hair of her head, and kissed his feet, and anointed them with the ointment (Lk. 7:37-38).

When the Pharisee sees Jesus' apparent approval of her actions, he doubts that He is an authentic prophet, for a real prophet would have known what kind of woman this is. Jesus responds with a parable about two debtors:

> A certain creditor had two debtors; one owed five hundred denarii, and the other fifty. When they could not pay, he forgave [*aphesis*] them both. Now which of them will love him more (Lk. 7:41-42)?

The story Jesus tells is a jubilee story, the story of the forgiveness of debt. The question of who will love more relates not simply to the parable, but to Simon and the woman.

Simon correctly answers Jesus' question: The one forgiven more will love more. Jesus then explains how His parable is a retelling of the story that has just unfolded before Simon's eyes: the story of generous, not stingy, love:

I entered your house, you gave me no water for my feet, but she has wet my feet with her tears and wiped them with her hair. You gave me no kiss, but from the time I came in she has not ceased to kiss my feet. You did not anoint my head with oil, but she has anointed my feet with ointment. Therefore I tell you, her sins, which are many, are forgiven [*apheontai*, from *aphesis*], for she loved much; but he who is forgiven little, loves little (Lk. 7:44-47).

Being forgiven, the woman is no longer bound to sin, but bound in gratitude to the holy prophet from Nazareth. Just as the debts were forgiven in the parable, so now are the sins of the woman. Indeed, the word that Jesus uses to declare the woman forgiven, *aphesis*, is the same word used in the jubilee legislation to describe the release from debt. Jesus transforms the jubilee release of debts into the release of sins. To be forgiven is to be released; forgiveness is freedom. The woman, now freed from the bondage of sin, goes forth in the *jubilation* that comes from encountering Christ.

Those at table, however, are not so jubilant. They find Jesus' declaration that the woman's sins are "released" hard to believe. They question among themselves, "Who is this, who even forgives sins" (Lk. 7:49)? Jesus had already been asked that question before, and He had answered it with an amazing action—the extraordinary healing of a paralytic.

Who Can Forgive Sins?

It was an event the little Galilean village would never forget. Word quickly spread that Pharisees and scribes from all over Galilee had come to hear the Nazarene who was said to be a mighty prophet and

healer, for the Spirit of God was with Him. As the
news spread, village residents gathered around the
house where teachers of the law were gathering to
hear Jesus.

Among those who heard the excited rumors and
gossip about this remarkable gathering was a group
of men with a paralyzed friend. As the rest of the village rushed over to catch a glimpse of the action, they
went out of their way to bring their friend forward for
a healing. Because the house was overflowing with
people pressing in to see what was happening, it was
impossible to carry the paralytic through the crowd
and into the house. One could well imagine the disap-
pointment of the man lying helpless on his bed. But
his friends did not give up. Refusing to let circum-
stances paralyze their resolve, they decided to make
things happen. Before the paralytic realized what was
going on, he was hoisted onto the roof of the house!

The men lowered the paralytic down through the
opening they made in the roof. Now all eyes are on
the man stretched out at Jesus' feet. What will the
prophet do? Seeing their faith, Jesus says to the paralytic, "Man, your sins are forgiven you" (Lk. 5:20). The
undaunted charity and faith of the paralytic's friends
result in more than a physical healing, as Jesus gives
the greater gift of forgiveness. The scribes and the
Pharisees who fill the room are scandalized: "Who is
this that speaks blasphemies? Who can forgive sins
but God only?" (Lk. 5:21). This would-be prophet
claims too much. God alone has the authority to forgive sins, and He established the Temple as the place
and its ritual sacrifices as the means to do it. But
now this prophet is claiming to be and to do what the

Temple was and did! To the guardians of Temple and Torah, Jesus is not only wrong, but blasphemous. Put simply, they do not believe that Jesus' words concerning forgiveness are effective, for who but God alone can forgive sins?

This gets to the point of the gathering. The Pharisees and scribes are there not to hear Jesus teach them, but to judge whether or not Jesus is a real prophet. In their minds, the claim to forgive sins does not prove that Jesus is a true prophet sent from God, but rather is evidence that this unorthodox teacher is far from being a legitimate prophet.

In prophetic fashion, Jesus reads their hearts and responds: "Why do you question in your hearts? Which is easier, to say, 'Your sins are forgiven you,' or to say, 'Rise and walk'" (Lk. 5:23)? Yes, Jesus admits, it is easy to tell the paralytic his sins are forgiven, since it is a spiritual matter and therefore invisible. Who can disprove His claim? But, to say to the paralytic, "Rise and walk," would be even more astonishing, since it is open to empirical investigation. Everyone will be able to judge for themselves the efficacy of such words.

> "But that you may know that the Son of man has authority on earth to forgive sins"—he said to the man who was paralyzed—"I say to you, rise, take up your bed and go home." And immediately he rose before them, and took up that on which he lay, and went home, glorifying God (Lk. 5:24-25).

Jesus clarifies the purpose of the healing: "that you may know that the Son of man has authority on earth to forgive sins" (Lk. 5:24). The healing functions as a sign. First, it confirms Jesus' claim to have divine authority to forgive sins. The miraculous action proves that extraordinary powers are at work in the man from Nazareth. Second, the physical healing manifests the spiritual healing effected by Jesus' forgiveness of sins. The man's immobility and paralysis signifies sin's crippling effect on the soul. When the paralytic rises at Jesus' word and walks with a newfound freedom, he illustrates visibly the greater freedom that he has been given through forgiveness of his sins.

Jesus' action is part of His jubilee program. Just as Jesus releases him from his sins—the word for forgiveness is once again *aphesis*, release—so too does He release him from his paralysis. This is the kind of action that Jesus announced He would do when He started His mission at Nazareth: "He has sent me to proclaim release (*aphesis*) to the captives . . . to set at liberty (*aphesis*) those who are oppressed" (Lk. 4:18).

Notice too that Jesus does not say to the man, "you are healed," but "Rise . . . and go home." The word for rise (*egeire*) is the same word used to describe Jesus' rising from the dead. Just as through sin death entered the world, so too, with forgiveness of sin, new life, and resurrection comes to those who follow Jesus. Certainly Luke and the early Christians who heard this story would see the connection. When Jesus forgives us our sins, we too "rise" and are able to "go home," home to the Father. Jesus' mission and healings signify the liberation, or exodus, which He is bringing about in order to lead us home. Carried in by the faith of his friends, the man now walks out of the house because of the release granted him by Jesus. As he makes his way through the astonished crowd, the man has become a walking witness to the jubilation that comes from encountering Christ.

Clean vs. Unclean

Jesus' healings are not simply random acts of power or pity, but are signs that inaugurate the good news of the kingdom of God. We should carefully contemplate the words that Jesus chooses to use in healing people, for they are often full of mystical meaning. In almost every case, Jesus does not simply declare the person healed, but tells them to "rise" or "be clean," or "be freed." The famous encounter between Jesus and the leper is a good example of how physical healing is intended by Jesus to point to something much deeper.

Leprosy was in Jesus' day what AIDS is today, a terrifying and deadly disease that often meant for its victim a life of suffering and abandonment.[1] In ancient Israel, anyone with leprosy was automatically exiled, by law, from his family and community, left to "dwell alone in a habitation outside the camp" (Lev. 13:46). Lepers were declared "unclean" (Lev. 13:11), which led to their being barred from the Temple and any participation in its liturgy. Lepers thus found

---

[1] In treating the healing of the leper, I owe much to my wife, Kris Gray, for her chapter "Sacraments of Healing: A Return from Exile and a Healing of Heart," in *Catholic for a Reason: Scripture and the Mystery of the Family of God* (Steubenville, OH: Emmaus Road Publishing, 1998), 261-86. She gives an excellent description of how Jesus' healings are symbolic of a return from exile. The physical healing points to the spiritual healing brought about by God's forgiveness of sins.

themselves exiled from family, society, and even the Temple where the Lord dwelt in the midst of Israel. Every leper yearned to be freed from the bondage and exile that his leprosy brought him.

While Jesus was visiting one of the many villages in Galilee, a leper throws himself down on his face before Him. According to the Torah, lepers were not to enter the village; they were quarantined from social contact. The leper must have heard about Jesus, as one can well imagine how fast rumors that a prophet had arisen would travel to those who were sick. Prophets like Elisha had been known for healing leprosy, and Jesus had already compared Himself to Elisha in His homily at Nazareth (cf. Lk. 4:27). Perhaps a family member or friend of the leper heard the rumors about Jesus and went to the out-skirts of the village to tell the leper of the good news. However the leper heard, he decided to act. He must have concealed himself in a cloak, since lepers were barred from entering the village, and quietly made his way through the crowd that gathered around Jesus to hear the Word of God. In a desperate gam-ble, the leper threw off his cloak, and cast himself at the mercy of this prophet from Nazareth. The crowd must have gasped, for Luke, who was a physician, tells us that the man was full of leprosy. One can only imagine how the advanced leprosy would have marred and completely disfigured his face and body. No part of him would be free of oozing sores and pus. Undoubtedly, the crowd would have retreated in repulsion. All stepped back in fear but one, the man whose mission it was to bring good news to the poor and oppressed.

The leper puts his petition plainly: "Lord, if you will, you can make me clean" (Lk. 5:12). Notice that the leper does not say, "Heal me." Surely, as the leper planned his approach to the prophet, he weighed what his words should be with great care. The nature of his request can escape our modern reading if we do not pay close attention to its wording and cultural context. The leper declares that he can be made "clean" if Jesus wishes. What the leper hopes and longs for is to be made "clean," and thereby ritually restored to the Temple and its liturgy. Not only does the leper demonstrate faith in Jesus but, if we understand him clearly, he shows a purity of intention that is as astonishing as his healing. More than the end of his social and physical exile, more than the end of his illness, the leper desires to end his liturgical exile and once again enter the house of the Lord to worship Yahweh and participate in Israel's liturgy.

The astonished crowd anxiously looks on to see what the man of God will do. Now it is Jesus' turn to surprise the crowd, for He responds by stretching out His hand to touch the leper! And as He touches him, He says, "I will; be clean" (Lk. 5:13). Anyone who was ritually unclean could not touch someone who was clean. If this happened, the clean would become unclean. The person who was clean and came into contact with the unclean would automatically be defiled and thereby barred from the Temple. Ritual washing, animal sacrifice, and other prescriptions had to be followed in order to be cleansed. Lepers could not legally be cleansed until their leprosy was healed and confirmed by the priests (Lev. 14). As the crowd gazes at the scene, they gasp in disbelief as the holy rabbi and prophet reaches out to touch the unclean leper.

But instead of Jesus' becoming unclean upon contact with the leper, the reverse happens. Jesus has brought a new power of purity that has not been seen in all of the Old Covenant. Now, when the clean and unclean clash, it is the unclean that is swallowed up in the clean. The power of the unclean, and all the sin, death, and defilement that it signifies, has been conquered in Christ. The leper experiences the return from exile, the new exodus that comes from encountering Christ.

In the Shadow of the Galilean

The encounter between the clean and unclean is behind many of Jesus' healings. Once we have an understanding of the cultural context of clean and unclean, which dominated the Jewish mindset of Jesus' day, we can make more sense of several otherwise strange encounters between Jesus and the sick. This is especially true for the woman who suffered from constant hemorrhaging.

The woman had suffered hemorrhaging for over twelve years. She had spent everything she had on physicians who could find no cure for her. One day, as Jesus is journeying to Jairus' house among a large crowd, she follows behind Him, hoping to be healed. Either too shy to make her request known among the crowd, or unable to present her petition to the prophet from Nazareth because of the multitude, she approaches Him from behind. Hurriedly pressing through the crowd despite her pain, she lunges forward to touch the holy teacher. Because of the dense crowd and the quick pace of the holy rabbi, her hand only grazes Him, and only her fingers faintly catch the "fringe of his garment" (Lk. 8:44).

Although she fails to catch hold of the holy man, the woman finds herself in the grip of grace, and her hemorrhaging is healed. For it is her faith, and not simply her fingers, that brush up against the source of grace. It is likely that many of the multitude touched Jesus that day, as Peter noted. But the grace and power of Jesus "went forth" (cf. Lk. 8:46) from Him at the touch of the woman alone. Why? Because she alone makes contact with Christ in faith; faith unlocks grace and unleashes the power of God's Anointed One.

Suddenly, however, Jesus stops and demands to know who had touched Him: "Who was it that touched me?" (Lk. 8:45). Peter, bewildered by Jesus' request to know who amongst the multitude had touched Him, exclaims, "'Master, the multitudes surround you and press upon you!' But Jesus said, 'Some one touched me; for I perceive that power has gone forth from me'" (Lk. 8:45-46). The woman, realizing that the prophet knows what had just occurred, falls down at His feet in fear. Why is she so afraid?

According to the Torah, the woman would have been ritually unclean because of her hemorrhaging (cf. Lev. 15:25). She knows that to touch someone would make him unclean, but in her desperation and faith she touched the teacher and prophet Jesus. Now He knew, and she expected to be rebuked. She falls in fear, trembling in terror of what the holy prophet might do. Rather than a rebuke, however, Jesus gently responds, "Daughter, your faith has made you well; go in peace" (Lk. 8:48).

Once again, the unclean is cured by the clean. Jesus' touch is transformative: Sickness turns into salvation, hurt into healing, and exile into exodus. The physical healing is a sign of the spiritual, the visible of the invisible. Thus, the mighty healings function as sacramental signs of the salvation that comes through Christ.

The Meaning Behind the Miracles

If Jesus is the Messiah, why does He spend so much time performing miraculous healings? What do the healings have to do with the new exodus that the Messiah was to bring about? What did Jesus intend to do by healing the blind, lame, and leprous?

The answers to these questions are essential for understanding the aims of Jesus' mission. When John the Baptist hears in prison about Jesus' mighty deeds of healing, he seems to be a bit puzzled.[2] It seems John expected that when the Messiah "gather[ed] the wheat" (Lk. 3:17) it would look different from Jesus' simple gathering of the sick and lame, the outcast and the poor. He may have expected the Messiah to come in a blaze of glory. Certainly the

---

[2] Jesus concludes His message to John with the words, "Blessed is he who takes no offense at me" (Lk. 7:23). Pope John Paul II, in commenting on these words, affirms that John the Baptist is a true and heroic prophet, but that he still needed to be reassured by Jesus: "These last words sound like a call, addressed directly to John, his heroic precursor, who had a different idea about the Messiah" (*Jesus: Son and Savior, Catechesis on the Creed*, Volume Two (Boston: Pauline Books, 1996), 127). By his petition to Jesus, John embodies the theological axiom of Saint Anselm, "faith seeking understanding."

Messiah, the new David, would set out to defeat the present-day Goliaths and begin His reign. Therefore, John the Baptist sends two of his disciples to Jesus, saying, "Are you he who is to come, or shall we look for another" (Lk. 7:19)?

When John's disciples reach Jesus, He happens to be very busy healing the blind, possessed, and diseased. In the midst of the healings, they deliver John's message. Jesus answers them:

> Go and tell John what you have seen and heard: the blind receive their sight, the lame walk, lepers are cleansed, and the deaf hear, the dead are raised up, the poor have good news preached to them (Lk. 7:22).

What kind of answer is that? Is that a yes or a no? It is a prophetic answer; prophet answering prophet, through an allusion to the words of another prophet, Isaiah.

Chapter 35 of Isaiah describes the new exodus that the Lord will accomplish, a kind of sneak preview of the good news that will be the announced in more detail in the second half of Isaiah. The good news begins, as in the famous chapter 40, in the wilderness. From there, the "glory of the Lord" is revealed. This revelation and new exodus will not be brought about in a blaze of glory, but in a remarkably different manner:

> Strengthen the weak hands,
>   and make firm the feeble knees.
> Say to those who are of a fearful heart,
>   "Be strong, fear not!" (Is. 35:3-4a).
> Then the eyes of the blind shall be opened,

> and the ears of the deaf unstopped;
> then shall the lame man leap like a hart,
> and the tongue of the dumb sing for joy (Is. 35:5-6).

As Pope John Paul II observed: "With this reply Jesus intended to confirm his messianic mission by referring in particular to the words of Isaiah (cf. Is. 35:4-5; 61:1)."[3] Jesus' answer to John the Baptist evokes the imagery of Isaiah's prophecy of the new exodus, the return from exile. Jesus' answer reminds John of Isaiah's account of the promised liberation of Israel, a new exodus marked by the healing of the deaf, blind, lame, and leprous. Jesus is saying, for those who have ears to hear, that His healings signify the new exodus; they shout out in a prophetic frequency that the Messiah has come, in the Person of Jesus.

Wasn't the Messiah supposed to bring liberation for Israel? According to the story, the new David was to gain glory by getting even with Goliath—so why isn't Jesus challenging the enemies of Israel? According to Luke, Jesus is playing the role of David, but the real Goliath is not Herod or Caesar, but Satan. And just as David defeated Goliath shortly after his royal anointing, Jesus defeated the devil in the desert, shortly after His anointing in the Jordan. Jesus is not sidestepping political liberation for the sake of an esoteric spiritual one. Rather, He is taking on the spiritual bondage and oppression first, since political liberation alone is but a caricature of genuine free-

---

[3] Pope John Paul II, *Jesus: Son and Savior, Catechesis on the Creed,* Volume Two, 127.

dom. His primary concern is the greater liberation from sin and evil. By releasing people from sickness, disease, and infirmity, Jesus is signifying, in a visible and physical way, the invisible and spiritual release He is accomplishing through the forgiveness of sins.

> In Jesus' eyes, healings are also a sign of spiritual salvation, namely liberation from sin. By performing acts of healing, He invites people to faith, conversion, and the desire for forgiveness.[4]

The healings are messianic signs, evidence that the kingdom of God has arrived in the Person of Jesus. It is the good news to the poor, and a sign of the liberation offered to those who follow in the shadow of the Galilean.

* * *

Questions for Reflection
or Group Discussion

1. (a) Why do you think that "those who are forgiven much, love much"? **(b)** Is Simon, or for that matter anyone, right in thinking that he is in need of only a little forgiveness? **(c)** Why does Jesus compare debt to sin, and its cancellation to forgiveness?

_____

_____

_____

---

[4] Pope John Paul II, *Mission of the Redeemer,* no. 14.

2. (a) In what ways are the physical effects of illnesses such as paralysis, leprosy, and other diseases similar to the spiritual effects of sin on the soul? **(b)** When we make petitions to the Lord like the leper, is our aim primarily for spiritual or earthly goods (cf. Catechism, nos. 2735-37)? **(c)** Do we understand what purity of intention is? Do we struggle to attain it?

_____

_____

_____

3. (a) Many people touched Jesus and yet never experienced the power of His grace like the woman healed from hemorrhaging. What made her encounter with Christ different from the others? **(b)** With her example in mind, why do our disposition and faith make a difference in receiving the fruits of God's grace offered to us in the sacraments, especially in receiving (touching) Christ in the Eucharist (cf. Catechism, no. 1128)?

_____

_____

_____

4. (a) What is the meaning behind Jesus' miracles of healing? **(b)** Why does Jesus respond to John's question by echoing Isaiah 35? In what ways is Isaiah 35 a key to unlocking the meaning of Jesus' miracles? **(c)** In what ways are Jesus' mighty deeds sacramental in nature? How do they use the visible to communicate the invisible, the physical to show forth the spiritual, and the earthly to illustrate heavenly realities?

4

THE NEW LAW
—LUKE 6—

J esus was known as "the teacher." What did He teach? The kingdom of God. The kingdom was the focus of His teaching, a teaching that took people by surprise and transformed the way they viewed the world. Jesus' teaching was not simply good advice but "good news." The good news was about an event, the advent of the kingdom of God. Through Jesus' words and deeds it became clear that He personally was bringing about the kingdom.

If we are to understand Jesus' teachings, we must put them squarely in the context of the kingdom. People were not gathering from all over Galilee to listen to a new prophet tell people to be nice. They came to hear a new king, the Messiah, lay down the new way of life for the new Israel. They came with the hope that Jesus would usher in a new kingdom, one that would replace the oppressive and corrupt rule of Caesar and his political puppet, Herod.

This context sheds great light on the significance of Jesus' famous speech in Luke, the "sermon on the plain" (cf. Lk. 6:17-49). Luke tells us that the night before the speech, Jesus called to Himself a large group of disciples, from whom He chose twelve leaders. The next day Jesus shocked His disciples and a multitude of people with a speech describing just what it means to be a part of the kingdom movement. We shall begin our analysis of His address by examining the perspective of those who gathered to hear the Galilean prophet.

The Seeds of Revolution

The motley group of men, gathered from all over Galilee, moved quickly along the rocky trails that lead up from the Sea of Galilee to the rising hill country. They had received word from the Master that they were to gather in the hills. What did this mean? They had seen the Master perform powerful prophetic signs of healing, preach and teach the multitudes in the surrounding villages, and proclaim the good news that the kingdom of God was at hand. He had awakened not only their attention, but the attention of all of Galilee, not to mention many leaders and officials from as far away as Jerusalem. Why was He calling them out into the hills? Was this the beginning of the kingdom? Was the prophet from Nazareth the Messiah who would marshal the men of Israel to reconquer Israel from her Roman and Herodian enemies?

In recent memory, about the time when Jesus was but an infant, Judas the Galilean had gathered a group of men around himself in the hills of Galilee in order to begin a revolutionary movement against Rome. The Romans quickly caught up with him and put him to death, scattering his rag-tag revolutionaries. Memories such as this made many wonder, as they wandered up the zigzagging paths, just what this gathering could mean. Anticipation grew with every step up the hilly terrain. Was the Nazarene the new David? And was He about to organize and lead the long-awaited revolution?

On one of the many hills of Galilee, the men from Galilee sat with Jesus. They had answered His summons with anticipation. Despite anxious inquiries, the Master said nothing of what was to happen, but spent the entire night in deep prayer. Wasn't this just like David, who would spend entire evenings and nights praying to the Lord? (cf. Ps. 6:6; 119:148). Finally, at dawn, the Master arose and called out to those gathered upon the hill. He looked intently upon the crowd, and calmly called out the names of twelve men whom He chose to be leaders. He named them *apostles*.

If anyone wondered whether Jesus was beginning to call for the kingdom, the choice of twelve leaders ended any doubts. The number twelve immediately called to mind the twelve tribes of Israel, which came forth from the twelve sons of Jacob, otherwise known as Israel. To choose twelve leaders made Jesus' intentions plain: Jesus was reconstituting Israel around Himself. The prophets foretold that the tribes would be reunited in the messianic time of renewal (cf. Jer. 31:10; Ezek. 20:41; 34:12; 2 Mac. 1:27). The calling of the twelve apostles shouted out in prophetic symbolism that the kingdom was at hand, and that Jesus was giving the marching orders.

Word must have spread that something momentous was about to happen. For, when Jesus came down from the hills to "a level place," not only was there a "great crowd of his disciples," but also a "great multitude of people from all Judea and Jerusalem and the seacoast of Tyre and Sidon," gathered together to hear what Jesus had to say, and many also came for healing (Lk. 6:17). The time could not be riper for the inauguration of the kingdom, for a revolution against Rome to begin. The people were ready for rebellion. All they lacked was the leadership. So, with rumors running wild, what would Jesus announce to the throng that thirsted for justice and hungered for freedom?

Paths to Happiness: The Beatitudes

Jesus begins His sermon with a blessing: "Blessed are you poor, for yours is the kingdom of God" (Lk. 6:20). Jesus addresses the multitude as "you poor." This fits the social context of Galilee in Jesus' day, where poverty "was a basic fact of life."[1] The economy of Galilee was largely agrarian. Paying taxes to Herod Antipas and to the Romans, in addition to the Temple tax and tithing, not to mention paying rent for one's land and house, made getting by a daily struggle. But to those who suffer and weep in their poverty, hunger, and persecution, Jesus promises consolation.

Jesus gives four blessings and then four woes; the woes are the inverse of the blessings. For example, those who hunger "shall be satisfied," while the full are warned that they "shall hunger" (Lk. 6:21, 25). The blessings and woes in Lk. 6:20-26 are purposely parallel, thereby emphasizing the correlation between them:

Blessings	Woes
Blessed are you poor, for yours is the kingdom of God.	But woe to you that are rich, for you have received your consolation.
Blessed are you that hunger now, for you shall be satisfied.	Woe to you that are full now, for you shall hunger.
Blessed are you that weep now, for you shall laugh.	Woe to you that laugh now, for you shall mourn and weep.
Blessed are you when men hate you . . . and revile you . . . for so their fathers did to the prophets.	Woe to you, when all men speak well of you, for so their fathers did to the false prophets.

Jesus takes the world's conception of what leads to happiness—riches, well-being, fame, and power—and turns it on its head. The more one pursues these things for the sake of happiness, paradoxically, the farther one will be from genuine happiness. Jesus' blessings and woes put the contrast between earthly and heavenly wisdom in stark focus. Why does Jesus seem to say that earthly goods are not sources of blessing? Because, as Saint Thomas keenly observed, "God alone satisfies" (Catechism, no. 1718; cf. Lk. 16:13). The beatitudes are radical because Jesus is giving a radical redefinition of what leads to happiness. The things of this world are not sufficient to satisfy the human heart. Only God can bring the fulfilling happiness for which we who are spiritually poor hunger.

Love Your Enemies

The lesson that God would fill the hungry with good things, while sending the rich away empty, is one that Jesus' audience would gladly hear. But before their thoughts can linger on images of Herod Antipas and his rich court being sent away empty, Jesus lays down a new law. "But I say to you that hear, Love your enemies, do good to those who hate you, bless those who curse you, pray for those who abuse you" (Lk. 6:27-28). If we simply take this as an abstract principle of universal love, we shall be draining Jesus' words of their historical life. His teaching is not the normal fare; far from serving

---

[1] Sean Freyne, *Galilee, Jesus, and the Gospels: Literary Approaches and Historical Investigations* (Philadelphia: Fortress Press, 1988), 160.

warmed-up leftovers, Jesus gives them fresh food
for thought. Jaws would drop, and not with a yawn.
These words do not settle upon the crowd like a
gentle breeze, but rather they sweep through the
audience like a hurricane. Why? The key to feeling
the force of Jesus' words is to try to hear them with
the ears of the poor who sat in His presence. Putting
these words in their historical context, they would
have sounded something like this to the Galileans
gathered together: "Love Herod and his minions, do
good to the Romans who hate you, bless their soldiers who curse you and abuse you." What kind of
revolution was this?

To those who lived under Roman rule, Jesus'
words had concrete and daily application. He drives
the point home: "To him who strikes you on the
cheek, offer the other also; and from him who takes
away your cloak do not withhold your coat as well"
(Lk. 6:29). You can almost hear the young Jewish
men gritting their teeth in disbelief. Jesus was not
speaking about hypothetical situations—many in the
crowd had probably suffered abuse from their oppres-
sors. If there were any hope that the prophet from
Nazareth would lead a resistance movement, those
hopes quickly dried up that day under the Galilean
sun. Vengeance and violence were not part of the
good news.

Imitating the Father

Undoubtedly the question would immediately
arise, why should they love the Romans? Jesus
quickly follows His exhortation to love enemies with
some motives for the apparent madness:

> If you love those who love you, what credit is that
> to you? For even sinners love those who love them.
> And if you do good to those who do good to you,
> what credit is that to you? For even sinners do the
> same (Lk. 6:32-33).

The people of Israel knew that they worshipped the
one true God and that by following His Torah they
were living by a higher standard than the Gentiles
did. So, playing on their religious pride, Jesus calls
them to a greater love:

> But love your enemies, and do good, and lend,
> expecting nothing in return; and your reward will be
> great, and you will be sons of the Most High; for he
> is kind to the ungrateful and the selfish (Lk. 6:35).

Jesus challenges His hearers. If they want to be
the true Israel, children of the Most High, then they
must imitate His mercy. The way of violent revolution may be the way of pagan gods and their Gentile
worshippers, but it was far from the Father's plan.
Jesus offers a different kind of revolution, a new way
of being Israel. This is the good news of the kingdom.

At the heart of Jesus' sermon is an axiom that is
the heartbeat of His whole kingdom ethic: "Be merciful, even as your Father is merciful" (Lk. 6:36). This
pithy proverb explains the injunctions to love one's
enemies and to do good to those who are abusive.
Jesus' explanation is strikingly similar to the one used
in the law of Moses. In the Torah, in what is known
as the Holiness Code, the reason for the entire moral
code is summed up in the phrase: "You shall be holy:
for I the LORD your God am holy" (Lev. 19:2). Israel

was to be holy, for her God was holy. Jesus echoes the Mosaic model, but with a twist. He drops the term "holy" and puts "mercy" in its place. Why? It is not that Jesus is downplaying the need for holiness, but rather clarifying it. Jesus opposes a view of God's holiness that was common in the first century: the vision of holiness proposed by the Pharisees.

The Politics of Holiness

The party of the Pharisees was the party of holiness. The term "holy" in Hebrew (*Qodesh*) literally meant set apart, separated. In fact, the name "Pharisee" was an Aramaic derivative of this term, and literally means separated (holy) one. The Pharisee party was the party of those who separated themselves from all that was unclean and non-Jewish. The Pharisees practiced a religion of quarantine to contain the unholy contagion of all uncleanness. They believed that imitating God's holiness meant separating oneself from everything and everyone who was unclean, especially sinners, tax collectors and, most of all, Gentiles. Jesus saw the dangerous nationalism engendered by this understanding of holiness. Thus He would later warn His disciples, "Beware of the leaven of the Pharisees" (Lk. 12:1).

Jesus had a different vision of God and therefore of ethics. The key to imitating God's holiness was mercy. The term for mercy in Hebrew, *hesed*, is a covenantal term. It was the steadfast love that was unconditional and obligatory for those bound by a covenant. It was a love that was as strong as death, for only death could annul a covenant. The old law had made mercy mandatory as well, but only upon those who were within the covenant: "You shall not take vengeance or bear any grudge against the sons of your own people, but you shall love your neighbor as yourself: I am the Lord" (Lev. 19:18). Those within the covenant boundary of Israel, "the sons of your own people," were to be loved and forgiven; but those outside the covenant were not included in the law. Jesus, however, radically redefined the boundary: Now, He was saying, you must show mercy (*hesed*) to all, even Gentiles.

The contrast between holiness as *hesed* and holiness as separation is the primary point behind the parable of the good Samaritan. Jesus tells the story of the good Samaritan to a lawyer who asks Jesus what he must do to inherit eternal life. Jesus in turn asks for his opinion, whereupon the lawyer answers with Deut. 6:5, love God with all your heart, along with the injunction "love your neighbor as yourself," from Lev. 19:18. After Jesus affirms this twofold summation of the law, love of God and neighbor, the lawyer makes an inquiry concerning the fine print: "And who is my neighbor?" (Lk. 10:29).

Embodying Mercy

The road that ran from Jerusalem to Jericho wound around countless hills, plunging up and down sharp ravines. The tough terrain that one had to traverse on this road provided golden opportunities for bandits and thieves to ambush. And this is what happened to the man in Jesus' story, who was suddenly jumped by a band of thieves. They beat him, stripped him, and left him bloodied and abandoned by the roadside, half dead.

> Now by chance a priest was going down that road;
> and when he saw him he passed by on the other
> side. So likewise a Levite, when he came to the
> place and saw him, passed by on the other side
> (Lk. 10:31-32).

Why do a priest and a Levite, both of whom were
coming down from Jerusalem where they probably
just served in the Temple, pass by the poor wounded
man?

The answer for their aversion of the dying man
would have been crystal clear to any Jew of the first
century. Both the priest and the Levite were well-
trained in the Torah and the rigorous ritual regulations of the Temple and, according to the law, any
contact with the dying man would have made them
ritually unclean (cf. Num. 19:11). If they became
unclean they were automatically barred from the
Temple. They would have to go through a series
of ritual prescriptions in order to be cleansed. The
whole process took, at the very least, an entire week
(Num. 19:11-19). The priest and Levite feared to face
the ritual consequences that could come through
contact with the bloodied body by the roadside.
Cautiously sidestepping the situation, they preserve
their threadbare notion of holiness, but at a price. Is
this the holiness that Yahweh yearns for?

> But a Samaritan, as he journeyed, came to where
> he was; and when he saw him, he had compassion,
> and went to him and bound up his wounds, pouring
> on oil and wine; then he set him on his own beast
> and brought him to an inn, and took care of him
> (Lk. 10:33-34).

The Samaritan has compassion on the Jewish man who was left for dead. The cultural context is crucial for understanding the story. Samaritans were hated by Jews. The Samaritans were the remnant of the ten tribes of Northern Israel that had been conquered by the Assyrians in 722 B.C. The Samaritans did two things that made them anathema to the Jews: They mixed their bloodline and their worship with the Gentiles. Such assimilation was the opposite of the separation that constituted holiness in the Jewish mindset. The Samaritans were viewed not simply with distrust, but disgust; they embodied the abandonment of holiness and the politics of separation. So, after a priest and Levite leave the man for dead, the astonishing part of the story is that a Samaritan is the one who has compassion on the Jewish man who lies dying.

The Samaritan embodies the Father's mercy. According to the old way of reading the law, one's neighbor was limited to "the sons of your own people." Now, Jesus makes the compelling case for a broader view of the law. Jesus then poses the question: "Which of these three, do you think, proved neighbor to the man who fell among the robbers?" The lawyer said, "The one who showed *mercy* on him" (Lk. 10:37).

And here is the irony of the story, for the priest and Levite were the literal kinsmen (neighbor) of the man, not the Samaritan. The politics of holiness had restricted the notion of neighbor, but mercy knew no limits. Jesus' teaching on holiness as mercy was a potent new wine, and it burst the old conceptions of holiness (cf. Lk. 5:37-39).

The Measure of Mercy

One of the first principles of the old law was the *lex talionis*: an eye for an eye, a tooth for a tooth. Far from intending to be cruel and harsh, the law sought to limit the escalation of violence. One could not be avenged sevenfold. The law also functioned to instill order through fear:

> And the rest shall hear, and fear, and shall never again commit any such evil among you. Your eye shall not pity; it shall be life for life, eye for eye, tooth for tooth, hand for hand, foot for foot" (Deut. 19:20-21).

The law of the *lex talionis* is simple, tit for tat; what you sow is what you will reap. Jesus takes this principle but reapplies it in a radically new way:

> Judge not, and you will not be judged; condemn not, and you will not be condemned; forgive, and you will be forgiven; give, and it will be given to you; good measure, pressed down, shaken together, running over, will be put into your lap. For the measure you give will be the measure you get back (Lk. 6:37-38).

Jesus refocuses the principle of *lex talionis*. Whereas in the old law the way was, "as you get, so you give back," the new law of Jesus makes the standard, "as you give, so will you be given." In both the old and the new it is "measure for measure," with this radical difference: In the old the measure was man, in the new it is God.

Before, the measure meted out is between people, it is a horizontal relation. But in the new, it is not simply a matter between two persons, one getting back what they dished out, for a third party is involved. Now the relation is vertical: What you do to others is what God will do to you. So if you show mercy, then God will show mercy to you. If you forgive others, God will forgive you. This subverts the old way, where one may think that it is just to strike those who have hit you. Now if you forgive them, then you can count on God's forgiveness. Jesus has given an interior dimension, a spiritual twist, to the principle of *lex talionis*. The model for morality is no longer how others treat you, but how you want to be treated by the Father. This is drilled in every time we pray the Our Father, for we petition the Father to "forgive us our sins, as we forgive those who are indebted to us." The word "as" is the key, for it reminds us that "the measure you give will be the measure you get back" (Lk. 6:38). Jesus therefore makes mercy the measure of the moral life.

It is hard enough to forgive a friend, but who on earth can forgive his enemy? Who? Jesus. He will not only talk the talk, but He will also walk the walk. And that walk will lead Him up Calvary, under the weight of the wood. Jesus' passion and death validates and confirms the sermon on the plain. On the Cross, Jesus embodies forgiveness; even though He is despised and rejected, the icon of the Father's mercy cries out from the Cross, "Father, forgive them; for they know not what they do" (Lk. 23:34). And He tells us, "Go and do likewise" (Lk. 10:37). The road to imitating the Father is by imitating the Son.

New Law for the New Covenant

In the Old Testament, it was Moses who came down from the mountain and delivered the old law. Now, Luke shows us, it is Jesus who comes down from the mountain (although some translations have Jesus going to the hills to pray, the Greek literally says "mountain"), and delivers the new law, which will be the *magna carta* of Jesus' New Covenant. This new law maps out the way to beatitude, to full human flourishing. It does not simply dictate a code for kingdom citizenship, but points to the way of life which makes one a son or daughter of the divine Father. Jesus is the new Moses, and His kingdom teaching is the new Torah. Jesus teaches that real holiness is not only a matter of separating oneself from sin, but also of cleaving to the merciful heart of the Father. The model is mercy, and such covenantal love—hesed—is to be given to all.

Whereas the Old Covenant was limited to ethnic Israel, the New Covenant is open to all people; it is universal (catholic). One is now bound to show mercy to all. Thus, Jesus takes the old notion of covenantal love and broadens it to fit into the New Covenant kingdom. This explains the astonishing call to love even the Romans, for they too are invited to the kingdom. Far from seeking to chase the Gentiles and Romans out of Israel, Jesus seeks to make them part of the new Israel. Jesus could beat them, but He would rather have them join Him, as children of the Father.

*   *   *

Questions for Reflection
or Group Discussion

1. (a) Jesus was a revolutionary, but how did His "revolution" differ from the revolution for which the people of Galilee had hoped? **(b)** Why did Jesus specifically choose twelve apostles? **(c)** What is symbolic about Jesus' giving the new law after coming down from a mountain?

_____

_____

_____

2. (a) In what ways are the beatitudes countercultural today? **(b)** Why does Jesus reject wealth, power, and fame as sources of happiness and blessing? **(c)** What is the one true source of happiness?

_____

_____

_____

3. (a) Why is Jesus' teaching about forgiveness of enemies so difficult for the Jews in Jesus' day? **(b)** Why is forgiveness still one of the most challenging aspects of Jesus' teaching today? **(c)** What is the motive that Jesus gives for forgiving others? **(d)** How does Jesus practice what He preaches?

_____

_____

_____

_____

4. (a) What was the Pharisees' view of holiness?
(b) What does the biblical notion of *hesed* mean?
(c) How does Jesus' view of holiness differ from
the Pharisees? **(d)** What is the measure of justice in
the Old Covenant? **(e)** How does Jesus change the
concept of *lex talionis*?

_____

_____

_____

_____

_____

5

SABBATH CONTROVERSIES
—LUKE 6, 13—

One of the most controversial aspects of
Jesus' ministry revolved around the sabbath.
Jesus' healings on the sabbath often sparked
heated debates with the religious leaders of Israel.
Why was the sabbath a flash point for the Pharisees?
What was the significance of the sabbath that it was
so jealously guarded by Israel's elite? And given the
fervor of the Pharisees concerning the sabbath, why
does Jesus provoke them by performing healings on
the holy day?

The Setting Sun on the Sabbath

All over the village of Capernaum, people stood
watching the sun slowly sink behind the hills. At
the edge of the village, on the still waters of the Sea
of Galilee, the last reflections of the sun's red disc
slowly shrank away; the hot day had finally ended.
With the sun hidden behind the hills, people quickly
left their homes and rushed over to Simon the fisher-
man's house. Earlier that day the whole village had
been gathered in the synagogue, and the man from
Nazareth, who many thought to be a prophet, came
and taught them with an authority and power they
had never heard before. After the synagogue service was over, He had gone down to Simon's house.
Rumor had it that the prophet from Nazareth could
heal, so at dusk all who where sick came to call at
Simon's (Lk. 4:40). With the sudden rush of people,
a large crowd had gathered at Simon's door. Why did
they all wait until sundown? The answer is that sun-

down marked the end of the sabbath day (the Jewish day was measured from sundown to sundown).

The sabbath was a sign of the covenant between Yahweh and Israel; to break the sabbath was to break the covenant (Ex. 31:12-17; Ezek. 20:20). In the Torah the sabbath is called a "sign" (Ex. 31:13), and in Old Testament times, as well as in Jesus' day, it carried considerable symbolic meaning. To observe the sabbath signified that one was a faithful Jew, whereas non-observance put one outside the covenant and outside Israel. According to the prophet Jeremiah, the failure to observe the sabbath was one of the key factors in the destruction of Jerusalem by the Babylonians (Jer. 17:19-27). This unfaithfulness brought upon Israel the covenant curses, one of which was exile. Sabbath observance was not simply a matter of personal piety; personal violation of the sabbath had national consequences.

Given this perspective, the zeal with which the Pharisees enforced the sabbath can be better understood. The scribes and the Pharisees were the guardians of the Torah, and the observance of the sabbath was one of their primary concerns. They were not out to promote legalism for its own sake; rather, they desired the renewal of Israel. The Pharisees knew that the breaking of the Torah led to the Babylonian exile and their present plight under Roman rule. They therefore believed it was going to take complete adherence to the Torah to bring Israel out of exile. Accordingly, the scribes and Pharisees emphatically taught that no work whatsoever was to be done on the sabbath. The sabbath was holy, set apart from the rest of the week.

In addition, given the Roman occupation of Israel and the pervasive influence of Greek culture, the sabbath grew in importance as it marked out Jewish identity in the midst of pagan and foreign domination. Sabbath observance was not simply a matter of custom; it was a matter of national and religious survival. Therefore, the sabbath and its prohibition from all work were guarded with great scrutiny by the guardians of Israel—the scribes and Pharisees—who oversaw the sabbath with religious fervor and political patriotism. Laxity in observing the sabbath was considered a denial of one's religious and social identity. In the eyes of the Pharisees, when the Jews disregarded the sabbath, they were jeopardizing the restoration of Israel.

This understanding of politics and the Torah fueled the Pharisees' zeal for the law. There is little wonder then why the sick and diseased waited until sundown—when the sabbath was over—to go to Simon's house for healing; no one would dare incur the wrath of their peers and especially of the Pharisees. No one, that is, but Jesus and His followers.

Spying out the Sabbath

Jesus and His disciples had been on a whirlwind tour of the synagogues of Galilee. In an effort to avoid the crowds and publicity, Jesus and His band left the main road and crossed through some grain fields, making their way to the next village. As they passed through the grain fields, the disciples were so hungry that they "plucked and ate some ears of grain, rubbing them in their hands" (Lk. 6:1). Immediately some Pharisees began to interrogate them, saying

"Why are you doing what is not lawful to do on the sabbath?" (Lk. 6:2).

The Pharisees unexpectedly appear in the story only after the sabbath infraction. Where did the Pharisees come from? Were they traveling with Jesus and His disciples? Unlikely. Or, were they spying on Jesus and His followers? Given that Jesus had become a public figure, one who was controversial and rapidly growing in fame, the guardians of Israel's Torah and identity likely felt it necessary to keep a close eye on this would-be prophet. And so when those who joined up with Jesus began to transgress the current teaching on the sabbath, up jumped the outraged Pharisees.

Jesus responds to the Pharisees' accusations with a story. He begins by asking these guardians of Scripture if they have ever read the story of David in 1 Sam. 21:

> Have you not read what David did when he was hungry, he and those who were with him: how he entered the house of God, and took and ate the bread of the Presence, which it is not lawful for any but the priests to eat, and also gave it to those with him? (Lk. 6:3-4).

In explaining the actions of His disciples, Jesus points to the actions of David and his men. Jesus suggests that to understand the present predicament of His hungry disciples, one must understand what happened to David and his band of men when they were traveling with an appetite and no food.

David had learned from his friend Jonathan, the son of King Saul, that Saul was seeking to kill David. David fled from the king, leaving everything behind.

He came to Nob, the city of the priests, in search of food and weapons. In dire urgency he asked the high priest, Ahimelech, for food. The high priest responded that he had no food, except the holy bread, the bread of the Presence. The bread of the Presence consisted of twelve loaves, which were set before the Lord in the sanctuary. This holy bread could not be eaten by anyone except the priests within the holy place (cf. Lev. 24:5-9). Ahimelech told David that he could have the consecrated bread, if only he and his men had "kept themselves from women" (1 Sam. 21:4). David responds:

> Of a truth women have been kept from us as always when I go on an expedition; the vessels of the young men are holy, even when it is a common journey; how much more today will their vessels be holy? (1 Sam. 21:5).

Ahimelech and David are alluding to the Old Testament tradition that the priests who ate consecrated bread had to refrain from marital relations for some period of time. Not only did the Old Testament priests practice continence during their Temple service but, as David pointed out to Ahimelech, so did the soldiers of Israel refrain from marital relations while on military service.[1] The soldiers of Israel were dedicated to Yahweh and the covenant, and they served in a sacrificial way similar to the priests.

For this reason, Ahimelech gave David and his men

---

[1] The parallels to the life of Christ and the apostles, not to mention the Catholic priesthood, are remarkable. If the holy bread of the Presence required holiness, how much more the holy bread of the New Testament, which is the Body and Blood of Our Lord!

the holy bread of the Presence, which was offered on the sabbath (Lev. 24:8). One of Saul's servants happened to witness Ahimelech aiding David. The servant, Doeg the Edomite, surreptitiously listened to the meeting between David and Ahimelech and reported it to Saul. In response, Saul has Ahimelech and all the priests, except Abiathar who escaped, put to death because of Doeg's report (1 Sam. 22:11-19).

Why does Jesus refer to this story of David, and how does it explain His disciples' actions? Mark Twain once observed that "history doesn't repeat itself, but it sure does rhyme." The rhyme of history discloses the reason, according to Jesus, for the disciples' apparent breaking of the sabbath. Just as David and his band of men had been pursued by the leaders of Israel, so too are Jesus and His band of men pursued by the modern leaders of Israel, the Pharisees. Since David and his men were following the priestly practice of continence, and because David was the Lord's anointed, they were granted the priest's privilege of eating the consecrated sabbath bread. By pointing to this Davidic precedent, Jesus is claiming that His men were free from the sabbath regulations by virtue of a priestly privilege.

Jesus' story is revealing. He is now in the role of David, and just as David traveled with a group of faithful men, pursued by the leaders of Israel, so too does Jesus. To those spying on the sabbath in a grain field, Jesus tells a story about David, his men, and another spy, named Doeg the Edomite. For those who have ears to hear, the rhyme between the two stories points to the reason for the disciples' actions. Jesus is the new David, who wanders all over Israel with the Sauls of Israel in pursuit.

Lord of the Sabbath

Jesus concludes His story about David with a bold claim: "The Son of man is lord of the sabbath" (Lk. 6:5). What does Jesus mean by "Lord of the sabbath"? It has often been understood that Jesus is claiming to have authority over and above the sabbath. It may be, however, that Jesus is doing more than simply asserting authority over the sabbath. He may be hinting that His lordship is especially related to the sabbath. In what ways does the sabbath relate to Jesus' lordship? Why does He call Himself the Lord of the sabbath?

The very next scene in Luke's Gospel takes up the issue of the sabbath and Jesus' exercise of lordship on—not over and against—the sabbath. On a sabbath day, Jesus entered a synagogue and began to teach. A man with a withered right hand happened to be present, "and the scribes and the Pharisees watched him, to see whether he would heal on the sabbath, so that they might find an accusation against him" (Lk. 6:7).

Jesus initiates an encounter by calling the man with the withered hand to come to the center of attention next to Him. With the man in full view, Jesus poses a question: "I ask you, is it lawful on the sabbath to do good or to do harm, to save life or to destroy it?" (Lk. 6:9).

The choice between doing good or harm, saving life or killing may seem rhetorical to us, but there is a good possibility that Jesus is making concrete reference to an exception to the sabbath law as taught by the Pharisees. What kind of exception would allow for harm and killing? Warfare. During the time of the Maccabean revolt, only a century and a half before the time of Jesus, a community of Jews was attacked on the sabbath day. Since it was the sabbath, they decided not to resist, lest they break the sabbath. Word quickly spread of the infamous sabbath slaughter, and Mattathias and his followers discussed what they should do, since the Gentiles were sure now to attack on only one day of the week.

> So they made this decision that day: "Let us fight against every man who comes to attack us on the sabbath day; let us not all die as our brethren died in their hiding places" (1 Mac. 2:41).

There was an exception made to the sabbath law: Warfare and killing were allowed for the sake of defense. So Jesus' question is more than a rhetorical one:

> The implied argument of Jesus was thus, "If it is lawful on the sabbath for the sake of Israel and the Torah to kill, how much more ought it be permitted to heal this man, who is an Israelite, on the sabbath!"[2]

They give no answer to Jesus, who then responds by commanding the man to stretch out his withered hand. He does so and it is restored. How do the Pharisees respond? "They were filled with fury and discussed with one another what they might do to

---

[2] Marcus J. Borg, *Conflict, Holiness and Politics in the Teachings of Jesus* (New York: Edwin Mellen Press, 1984), 159.

Jesus" (Lk. 6:11). The irony is thick; by their actions the Pharisees have answered Jesus' question, for they condemn His healing on the sabbath while on that very day they also plan His destruction. For them it is lawful to harm and kill, but not to heal and cure.

The Lord of the sabbath restored the man's hand in the sight of all. It is noteworthy that the man did not request to be healed; it was Jesus who initiated the healing. Certainly Jesus knew that such sabbath activity would create controversy. Why does He seem to go out of His way to stir up the Pharisees by healing on the sabbath?

The Sabbath and Israel's Exodus

On another occasion, Jesus is teaching in a synagogue on the sabbath. In the audience is a woman who could not fully straighten herself, because she has had "a spirit of infirmity for eighteen years" (Lk. 13:11). Out of compassion Jesus calls out to her and says, "Woman, you are *freed* from your infirmity" (Lk. 13:12). Just as in the case of the man with the withered hand, Jesus initiates the healing. What makes this pattern so remarkable is that in every healing that Jesus performs on a day other than the sabbath, it is always those who are sick, or their friends, who initiate the healing. The leper beseeches Jesus, the friends of the paralytic bring him before Jesus, and the hemorrhaging woman reaches out to touch Jesus. But on the sabbath no one comes to Jesus requesting to be healed. Rather, on these occasions Jesus initiates the healings. It seems that Jesus prefers to heal on the sabbath.

The ruler of the synagogue responds to the healing with indignation. He does not have the courage to rebuke the powerful prophet from Nazareth for healing on the sabbath. Instead, he reprimands the people, saying, "There are six days on which work ought to be done; come on those days and be healed, and not on the sabbath day" (Lk. 13:14). The synagogue ruler is referring to the third of the Ten Commandments, which begins:

> Remember the sabbath day, to keep it holy. Six days you shall labor, and do all your work; but the seventh day is a sabbath to the LORD your God; in it you shall not do any work (Ex. 20:8-10).

Jesus does not sit passively by, however, but instead comes to the defense of the people:

> You hypocrites! Does not each of you on the sabbath *untie* his ox or his ass from the manger, and lead it away to water it? And ought not this woman, a daughter of Abraham whom Satan *bound* for eighteen years, be *loosed* from this *bond* on the sabbath day? (Lk. 13:15-16).

Jesus makes a common-sense argument: If it is allowable to untie an ox or ass on the sabbath in order to lead it to water, how much more ought this daughter of Abraham be loosed from her bondage!

In His response, Jesus not only reprimands the ruler of the synagogue and the Pharisees, but also gives us an insight into what His healings are all about. The loosing of the ox and the ass is analogous to the loosing of the woman from the bonds of Satan. Jesus emphasizes the symbolic nature of His deed by telling the woman that she is "freed," rather than simply declaring that she is "healed." Jesus sees His healing as an act of liberation, hearkening back to the start of His mission when He announced that He was to "set at liberty those who are oppressed," and to "proclaim release to the captives" (Lk. 4:18). Jesus' mighty miracle is a jubilee deed, for it brings liberty to one whom "Satan bound" (Lk. 13:16).

Why does Jesus seem to suggest that the sabbath is actually the most appropriate time for the woman to be released? The reason may be that the purpose of the sabbath is the remembrance of the release and subsequent rest from Egyptian servitude:

> You shall remember that you were a servant in the land of Egypt, and the LORD your God brought you out thence with a mighty hand and an outstretched arm; therefore the LORD your God commanded you to keep the sabbath day (Deut. 5:15).

Israel was in bondage in Egypt, and the exodus was the event that liberated Israel from bitter slavery. The sabbath was the sign of the exodus, a day of rest from labor. The sabbath rest symbolized the rest that the Israelites experienced in their liberation from Egyptian bondage. Since the sabbath commemorates the liberation of the exodus, what better day to heal, and thus liberate the oppressed, than on the sabbath? Thus Jesus uses the celebration of the exodus and subsequent covenant to proclaim a new exodus and the New Covenant.

The reason Jesus heals on the sabbath is not to enrage or even to tweak the Pharisees and their followers, but rather to highlight the sabbath-significance of His mission. Jesus followed the prophetic tradition of Israel, in which prophets would carry out a highly symbolic action in order to deliver a powerful message. The timing of such an action could underscore its symbolic import. A modern American example would be the dumping of tea on the fifteenth of April, the date on which income tax is due, to signify that taxes are unfair and burdensome in a manner that calls to mind the famous Boston Tea Party.

Could it be coincidental that all the healings that Jesus initiates happen to occur on the sabbath? Jesus made the sabbath a "prime time" for His miraculous healings in order to highlight their meaning. The divine physician worked to release people on the sabbath, to give them the liberation and rest which the sabbath commemorated. The sabbath was the commemoration of Israel's liberation from bondage, and now Jesus, ushering in the new exodus, announces that those bound by Satan are freed.

The sabbath context provides the interpretative backdrop to Jesus' sabbath healings. The sabbath commemorates the exodus; the sabbath rest is a reminder of the rest Israel experienced after being freed from slavery in Egypt. Thus the sabbath is a perpetual celebration and reminder of the exodus. Indeed, the very commandment that mandates the sabbath rest reveals how its observance is for the purpose of remembering the exodus:

> You shall remember that you were a servant [slave] in the land of Egypt, and the LORD your God brought you out thence with a mighty hand and an outstretched arm; therefore the LORD your God commanded you to keep the sabbath day (Deut. 5:15).

Jesus is leading a new exodus. He is the Messiah who has come to liberate Israel. This time it is not Pharaoh, but Satan, who holds God's people enslaved and "bound." When Jesus performed His first sabbath healing in having the man stretch forth his hand, He may have intended to evoke Deut. 5:15, which explains that the sabbath commemorates God's bringing about the exodus with "a mighty hand and an outstretched arm."

The significance of the sabbath in Jesus' ministry fits perfectly with Jesus' jubilee mission, which according to Isaiah was "to proclaim release to the captives" and "to set at liberty those who are oppressed" (Lk. 4:18). Jesus' sabbath deeds, far from being dissonant with the sabbath, are in complete harmony with it, which is why He is the "Lord of the sabbath."

*   *   *

Questions for Reflection
or Group Discussion

1. (a) Why were the Pharisees so zealous about the sabbath? **(b)** What motivated their zeal for the Torah and particularly the sabbath?

_____

_____

_____

2. (a) Why do you think the Pharisees were spying on Jesus and His disciples, as seems to be the case when they caught the disciples plucking grain on the sabbath (Lk. 6:1-5)? **(b)** Why does Jesus tell the story of David's flight from Saul to the Pharisees? **(c)** What are the parallels between these episodes in the lives of David and Jesus? **(d)** In the story from 1 Samuel 21-22, whom do the Pharisees parallel?

_____

_____

_____

_____

_____

3. (a) According to Deuteronomy 5:15, what does the sabbath commemorate? **(b)** Why do you think Jesus initiates healing only on the sabbath? **(c)** Explain how the sabbath provides a backdrop to Jesus' sabbath healings. **(d)** What is the symbolism of Jesus' telling the woman bent over with infirmity for eighteen years that she is "freed," as opposed to telling her she is "healed" (Lk. 13:12)? **(e)** Why does Jesus call Himself "the Lord of the sabbath"?

_____

_____

_____

_____

_____

6

JOURNEY TO JERUSALEM
—LUKE 9-19—

The central section of the Gospel of Luke consists of ten chapters known as the "travel narrative." This narrative begins with Jesus' setting "his face to go to Jerusalem" (Lk. 9:51) and runs all the way to the end of chapter nineteen, where Jesus finally enters the holy city. Luke's central section brims over with Jesus' teachings in the form of parables, sayings, and verbal exchanges with the Pharisees. At several points in the narrative, Luke emphasizes that these teachings are given in the context of Jesus' final journey to Jerusalem: "He went on his way through towns and villages, teaching, and journeying toward Jerusalem" (Lk. 13:22). That Jesus gives this teaching as He makes His way to Jerusalem provides a key to understanding the significance of His teachings.

Indeed, one of the striking themes of Jesus' parables is the "coming" of the master to his estate, whereupon he rewards the servants he finds ready and faithful and punishes the unprepared. The theme of "coming" found throughout Jesus' stories and sayings hints at lessons that have real-life application in His own "coming" to Jerusalem. When we examine Jesus' teaching in light of His coming to Jerusalem, both become mutually interpretive, thereby shedding further light on Jesus' messianic mission.

Transfiguring Sinai

The Transfiguration is the event that sets Jesus off to Jerusalem. Shortly after the Transfiguration, Jesus "set his face to go to Jerusalem" (Lk. 9:51). What is it about the Transfiguration that turns Jesus' attention to Jerusalem? What is so pivotal about this amazing and seemingly bizarre event that makes it the hinge of the story, leading Jesus onto a road that will end on Calvary?

The disciples were still reeling from the shocking challenge that Jesus had given them the prior week. In response to Peter's confession that Jesus was the "Christ of God" (Lk. 9:20), the Messiah, Jesus had said some shocking things about what it meant to follow Him: "If any man would come after me, let him deny himself and take up his cross daily and follow me" (Lk. 9:23). The notion of carrying one's cross meant only one thing in first-century Israel: Roman execution. The Roman penalty for rebellion was crucifixion, which entailed carrying the crossbeam to the place of one's execution, usually by a main road or thoroughfare where many could witness what happens to those who rebel against Rome. To be challenged to "take up one's cross" was disquieting to say the least. No wonder then that Jesus decided to take some of the disciples on a retreat.

About eight days later Jesus took Peter, James, and John up Mount Tabor to pray. At the top of the mountain, as they are praying, all heaven breaks loose. It starts with Jesus' face, which begins to glow with glory. Not only His face, but "his raiment became dazzling white" as well (Lk. 9:29). Then Moses and Elijah appear. The three disciples then behold Jesus speaking with Moses and Elijah. What did Jesus discuss with Moses, the giver of the Torah, and Elijah, the great prophet? Luke alone discloses the content of their conversation. They "spoke of his *departure* [literally *exodus* in Greek], which he was to accomplish at Jerusalem" (Lk. 9:31). Whom better to discuss the exodus with than Moses, the leader of Israel's first exodus?

Seeing Jesus' glory, not to mention Moses and Elijah, is enough to wake up Peter and his companions, who are probably exhausted from the climb up the mountain. Peter then makes what seems to be a very odd suggestion: "Master, it is well that we are here; let us make three booths, one for you and one for Moses and one for Elijah" (Lk. 9:33). Does Peter want to set up camp on the holy mount?

Luke has given us a clue to what Peter is thinking when he mentions that this event took place on the eighth day (Lk. 9:28). In the Jewish liturgical calendar, there is one feast that lasts eight days, the Feast of Tabernacles (Lev. 23:36). This feast commemorates the exodus and particularly the giving of the law on Sinai. On the eighth day of the feast, booths are set up to commemorate how the Israelites lived in tents during the exodus. It is possible that they went up the mountain to pray that day because it was the solemn high day of the Feast of Tabernacles. What better place to remember Sinai than on a mountain?

Indeed, the events of Sinai are not only remembered but also repeated during the Transfiguration. The glory cloud of the Lord descends upon the mount and the disciples who, like the Israelites of old, are afraid. "And a voice came out of the cloud, saying, 'This is my Son, my Chosen; listen to him!'" (Lk. 9:35). The following chart illustrates the striking parallels between Sinai and the Transfiguration:

Sinai	Transfiguration
(Ex. 24:15) "up on the mountain"	(Lk. 9:28) "up on the mountain"
(Ex. 24:15) Moses	(Lk. 9:30) Moses
(Ex. 24:16) glory cloud	(Lk. 9:34) glory cloud
(Ex. 24:18) "Moses entered the cloud"	(Lk. 9:34) "they entered the cloud"
(Ex. 24:16) voice calling out from cloud	(Lk. 9:35) voice calling out from cloud
(Ex. 34:30) people afraid	(Lk. 9:34) disciples afraid
(Ex. 34:29) Moses talks with God	(Lk. 9:30) Moses talks with Jesus
(Ex. 34:29) Moses' face shines with glory	(Lk. 9:29) Jesus' face shines with glory

On Mount Sinai, Moses' face was transfigured with the glory of God. Jesus' face also shines with glory, but even more than Moses, Jesus' whole appearance becomes "dazzling white" (Lk. 9:29). Jesus outshines Moses in reflecting the glory of the Lord. The connection with Moses' transfiguration shows that Jesus' transfiguration in glory is not simply a manifestation of His divinity, but rather a revelation of Jesus' perfected and glorified humanity. Jesus reveals God the Father's desire to transform humanity into the likeness of divine glory. This makes sense once we consider that when Moses radiated God's glory it was not a sign that Moses was divine, but rather that he was granted the grace to share in God's glory. The aim of the transfiguration is not simply to give a glimpse of Jesus' divinity, but to give us a glimpse of true humanity, a humanity that reflects the image and likeness of God in glory.

The events of Sinai are transfigured by the descent of glory upon Jesus on Tabor. On the mount of Transfiguration—the new Sinai—a new Torah is revealed. The new Torah is not the word of God written on stone tablets, but the Word made flesh. The voice from the cloud announces the new law, which is a person: "This is my Son, my Chosen; listen to him!" (Lk. 9:35). On the new and greater Sinai, the Father reveals His Son. Jesus takes the place of the Torah, not that the Torah is abolished, but now that the sun has come it is time to blow out the candles. Jesus embodies the Torah; the best way to know and understand the will of the Father is to look at and listen to His Son. The command, "listen to him" (Lk. 9:35), echoes the poignant prophecy of Moses that one greater than he would come and give a new covenant and law, and Moses concluded the prophecy with the injunction that Israel listen to Him (cf. Deut. 18:15-18).[1] Jesus is that new and greater Moses.

The conversation among Moses, Jesus, and Elijah concerns Jesus' exodus. The connection with Moses highlights how Jesus' mission is to be seen as a new exodus. The place for the exodus is Jerusalem. Shortly after this conversation, Jesus "set his face to

---

[1] In Deut.18:15, Moses says, "The LORD your God will raise up for you a prophet like me from among you, from your brethren—him you shall *heed*." The word "heed" translates the Hebrew word for "listen," which makes the words in Lk. 9:35, "listen to him," an exact parallel. The RSV translates the word "listen" as "heed" because in Hebrew to listen is to obey.

go to Jerusalem" (Lk. 9:51). The reason is revealed on Tabor: Jesus is journeying to Jerusalem to accomplish the new exodus. The mission of the Messiah comes into stark focus on the mount of Transfiguration. There would be no turning back.

Prophetic Mission

The unusual phrase, "set his face to go to Jerusalem," is a Hebrew idiom used to describe the arduous mission of a prophet. Prophets were often given the difficult task of delivering what at best was an unpopular message, such as notifying people of their sins and warning them of impending judgment. One wanted to see a prophet about as much as one wanted to see a dentist without painkillers. The idea of setting one's face signified having the resolve to carry out a mission despite its likely resistance and rejection, which often meant for the prophet being prepared for the worst, like Isaiah's being sawed in half.

The prophet most like Jesus in this regard was Ezekiel. He was instructed to give a message of threat, warning, and doom to the Temple, Jerusalem, and the people of Israel. The Lord encouraged Ezekiel to keep his resolve, exhorting him to set his face to Jerusalem: "Son of man, *set your face toward Jerusalem* and preach against the sanctuaries; prophesy against the land of Israel" (Ezek. 21:2).

Ezekiel, interestingly enough, was called by Yahweh "the son of man," a title Jesus takes up for Himself. The parallels between Jesus and Ezekiel are truly striking. Ezekiel was sent to warn and admonish Israel of impending judgment. Ezekiel set his face to

Jerusalem and the Temple and foretold their destruction. Ezekiel was told that the people will "hear what
you say but they will not do it" (Ezek. 33:31). Jesus
too gives prophetic warning to the people and predicts the impending destruction of Jerusalem and the
Temple. Ezekiel foretold the destruction of the first
Temple, Jesus the second.

Woven throughout Jesus' teaching in the travel narrative are prophetic warnings and admonishments to
repent. For example, at one time along the way some
people come up to Jesus and tell Him about "the
Galileans whose blood Pilate had mingled with their
sacrifices" (Lk. 13:1). Jesus responds that they did
not suffer their fate because they were worse sinners
than other Galileans. "I tell you, No; but unless you
repent you will all likewise perish" (Lk. 13:3). He also
mentions the eighteen who perished when the tower
of Siloam fell upon them. Again, He asserts that they
were not worse than any in Jerusalem, but "unless
you repent you will all likewise perish" (Lk. 13:5).

Jesus uses these catastrophic events as examples of
what will befall the people of Galilee and Jerusalem
unless they repent. Two provocative signs are given: a
bloody sacrifice at the hands of the Romans and death
by falling rubble. Both foreshadow the horrific events
that will befall both Galilee and Jerusalem in about
forty years, during the Jewish revolt against Rome.

Jesus follows His admonishment to repent with a
parable. A man planted a fig tree in a vineyard, and
when he came seeking fruit, it bore none. He said to
his vinedresser, "Lo, these three years I have *come*
seeking fruit on this fig tree, and I find none" (Lk.
13:7). The man then gave orders that the tree be cut

down, but the vinedresser convinced him to wait one more year to see if it would bear fruit.

Given that John the Baptist had already warned the multitudes to "[b]ear fruits that befit repentance," and threatened that "every tree therefore that does not bear good fruit is cut down and thrown into the fire" (Lk. 3:8-9), Jesus probably juxtaposed this parable about fruit with His warnings about repentance intentionally. Some commentators have even seen the reference to the man's seeking fruit for three years as a reference to Jesus' public ministry's lasting three years. In addition, the vineyard was a symbol of the nation of Israel in the prophetic writings (e.g., Hos. 9:10). Thus the fig tree that fails to bear fruit stands for Israel's lack of repentance. It is worth noting that Jesus tells a story about a man who comes to a vineyard seeking fruit, as He Himself is coming to Jerusalem, especially since Jerusalem is depicted by Isaiah as a vineyard that fails to bear fruit (Is. 5:1-7).

The Coming Judgment

The motif of "coming" is one of the major themes of the travel narrative. Many of Jesus' parables have as their subject the "coming" home of the master of the house, and the subsequent judgment that ensues. An excellent example is the parable of the marriage feast. Notice how many times the word "come" occurs:

> Let your loins be girded and your lamps burning, and be like men who are waiting for their master to *come* home from the marriage feast, so that they may open to him at once when he *comes* and knocks. Blessed are those servants whom the master finds awake when he *comes*; truly, I say to you, he will gird himself and have them sit at table, and he

will *come* and serve them. If he *comes* in the second watch, or in the third, and finds them so, blessed are those servants! But know this, that if the householder had known at what hour the thief was *coming*, he would have been awake and would not have left his house to be broken into. You also must be ready; for the Son of man is *coming* at an hour you do not expect (Lk. 12:35-40).

Five times the coming of the master is mentioned, one time the coming is described as that of a thief, and all the comings are shown to be illustrations of the "coming" of Jesus, the Son of man. The "coming" of the thief is compared to the master's coming in order to highlight the readiness needed for the unexpected arrival. The sudden "coming" of the master brings about a reckoning; reward and punishment are dealt out according to conduct. The servants who are ready to receive the master when he comes will "sit at table" and the master "will come and serve them" (Lk. 12:37). The servants who fail to "make ready or act according to his will" are severely punished (Lk. 12:47). Readiness for the master's coming is a common theme in Jesus' travel narrative teaching.

When Jesus draws near to Jerusalem, He tells another story about the return of a master and the subsequent reckoning that his servants receive. The story begins with a nobleman setting out to a far country in order to receive kingly power. This may seem odd to modern ears, but it would have been quite familiar to those who lived in the Roman Empire. Rome allowed local kings (e.g., Herod) to rule in various parts of the Roman Empire, but they received their power from Rome and remained subject to Rome. The nobleman entrusts ten of his servants with a talent and instructs them, "Trade with these till I *come*" (Lk. 19:13). The citizens subject to the nobleman send an envoy to the far country, requesting that the nobleman be denied his kingship, for they do not want him to rule over them.

Despite this petition, the nobleman returns with kingly power and commands his servants to give an accounting of their talents. The first two servants are rewarded for their faithfulness and granted a share in the kingdom's rule. But the third fails to make any increase in his talent, and gives his talent back to his "Lord" (Lk. 19:20). The nobleman had given the talents with the warning that he would "come" to receive their fruit (Lk. 19:13). In his dialogue with the unfaithful servant, the master recalls the earlier warning by repeating the motif of "coming," declaring to the unfaithful servant that "at *my coming* I should have collected it with interest" (Lk. 19:23).

It is no mere coincidence that, as Jesus makes His way to Jerusalem and the Temple, He tells stories about a master's returning to his house. Indeed, the primary title by which the disciples address Jesus in the Gospel of Luke is "master" (Gk. *kyrios*), which is also translated as "lord." The correlation is clear: Jesus is telling stories about a master (lord) who is returning to his home and checking up on the stewards. Just as in His parables, Jesus too is coming home to check up on the stewards of God's house. Blessing and woe are dealt out according to one's reception of Jesus. The parables are telling the story of Jesus; the lord is coming home.

The Coming Storm

Jesus knows that His coming will cause division. "Do you think that I have *come* to give peace on earth? No, I tell you, but rather division" (Lk. 12:51). Then He compares the present time to the coming of a storm:

> When you see a cloud rising in the west, you say at once, "A shower is *coming*"; and so it happens. . . . You know how to interpret the appearance of earth and sky; but why do you not know how to interpret the present time? (Lk. 12:54, 56).

The coming of Jesus to Jerusalem is compared to a coming storm, and few perceive the storm clouds gathering on Jerusalem's horizon.

The motif of coming, master, house and Jerusalem are brought together in a brief incident when Jesus is warned of Herod's plans to kill Him. The Pharisees warn Jesus to flee from Galilee because Herod desires Jesus' death.[2] Since Herod has jurisdiction only over Galilee, while Pilate is governor of Judea and Jerusalem, the Pharisees suggest that Jesus flee to Jerusalem for safety. Jesus is undeterred, and replies, "Nevertheless I must go on my way today and tomorrow and the day following; for it cannot be that a prophet should perish away from Jerusalem" (Lk. 13:33). Jesus observes that Jerusalem is hardly the place for a prophet to find safety, and then Jesus begins a lament over Jerusalem:

---

[2] It is interesting to note that when Pilate hands Jesus over to Herod, Herod sends Jesus back. If Herod, as the Pharisees claimed, was really seeking to kill Jesus, it is odd that he would release Jesus back to Pilate instead of executing Him.

> O Jerusalem, Jerusalem, killing the prophets and stoning those who are sent to you! How often would I have gathered your children together as a hen gathers her brood under her wings, and you would not! Behold, your house is forsaken. And I tell you, you will not see me until you say, "Blessed is he who *comes* in the name of the Lord!" (Lk. 13:34-35).

Jerusalem is told that her house—i.e., the Temple—is "forsaken." This is an ominous foreshadowing of the poor state in which Jesus will find the Lord's house when He comes to Jerusalem. Jesus predicts that Jerusalem will not see Him until they sing the refrain of Ps. 118, which gives a benediction to the one "who enters in the name of the LORD" (Ps. 118:26). This refrain, called the *Benedictus*, is now part of the *Sanctus* (Holy, Holy, Holy) at Mass. It will be sung during Jesus' triumphal entry into Jerusalem. Jesus' response gives a clear answer to John the Baptist's earlier question, "Are you he who is to *come*, or shall we look for another?" (Lk. 7:19). There is no need to look for another, for Jesus is the master (Lord) who is coming.

Royal Entrance

Jesus makes a royal entrance into Jerusalem. He begins by sending two disciples into a nearby village to obtain a colt. They are instructed by Jesus to tell the owners that "[t]he Lord has need of it" (Lk. 19:31). The title "Lord" paints Jesus in a royal portrait. This royal stature is further colored by the subsequent events of Jesus' entry into Jerusalem. Riding into Jerusalem on a colt is reminiscent of the royal son of David, Solomon, who rode a donkey in his enthronement procession into Jerusalem (1 Kings 1:38-40). It also hearkens back to Zechariah's famous prophecy that the Messiah would humbly ride into Jerusalem on a donkey (cf. Zech. 9:9). When the crowds spread their garments on the road before Jesus, they are making a public profession that He is their king, as the Israelites of old had done to Jehu when he was made king (2 Kings 9:13). Then they climactically call out, "Blessed is the King who *comes* in the name of the Lord!" (Lk. 19:38; cf. Ps. 118:26). This psalm had been one of the enthronement songs of ancient Israel, sung as the king processed into Jerusalem and the Temple. Now Jesus is the King who comes to the capitol, and He heads straight for the Temple.

The imagery of one coming to the Temple in the name of the Lord evokes an important prophecy of the Old Testament. The last prophet of the Old Testament, Malachi, foretold that "the Lord whom you seek will suddenly *come* to his temple" just after a messenger is sent to prepare the way of the Lord (Mal. 3:1). This coming is fraught with danger: "[B] ehold, he is coming, says the LORD of hosts. But who can endure the day of his *coming*, and who can stand when he appears?" (Mal. 3:1-2). The day of His coming was to be marked by judgment, especially upon the priests, the "sons of Levi" (Mal. 3:3). According to Malachi, the chief accusation that the Lord will have against them is that they rob God: "Will man rob God? Yet you are robbing me" (Mal. 3:8). In light of this prophecy, Jesus' charge against the Temple, "My house shall be a house of prayer; but you have made it a den of robbers," makes prophetic sense (Lk. 19:46; cf. Jer. 7:11). Jesus is the Lord who comes suddenly to the Temple and finds that the stewards of His house have been unfaithful.

A few days after this incident, Jesus delivers a prophetic message of doom to the Temple. Upon hearing some of His disciples praising the beauty and dignity of the Temple, Jesus announces its imminent end: "As for these things which you see, the days will come when there shall not be left here one stone upon another that will not be thrown down" (Lk. 21:6). The disciples immediately ask Jesus when this will be, and what signs will herald its fall. Jesus answers with a disturbing discourse that details the cataclysmic events surrounding the Temple's destruction, such as pestilence, earthquakes, and war. The telltale sign will be "when you see Jerusalem surrounded by armies, then know that its desolation has come near" (Lk. 21:20). Jesus then advises:

> [L]et those who are in Judea flee to the mountains, and let those who are inside the city depart, and let not those who are out in the country enter it; for these are days of vengeance, to fulfil all that is written (Lk. 21:21-22).

Jesus gave a definite timetable: "Truly, I say to you, this generation will not pass away till all has taken place" (Lk. 21:32). Jesus prophesied the destruction of the Temple within a generation, and history proved Him right, for the Temple was utterly destroyed, along with Jerusalem, during the Jewish revolt against Rome some forty years later (70 A.D.).

The early Christians took Jesus' prophecy concerning the destruction of the Temple and Jerusalem very seriously. According to Eusebius, an early

Christian historian, all the Christians knew the prophecies of Jerusalem's demise and so they fled from Jerusalem before it was besieged by the Romans.[3] It is interesting to note that the Acts of the Apostles, the sequel to Luke's Gospel, recorded that the early Christians in Jerusalem sold all their property (Acts 4:32-35). No other Christian community, whether in Antioch or Ephesus, is known to have done the same, even though they were strong in charity. Why did they sell their property? Because they knew from Jesus' prophecy that the real estate value in Jerusalem was soon to plummet. They sold their property and shared the burden of the move out of Jerusalem among the entire community.

Many believe that Jesus was not simply speaking of the end of the Temple, but of the entire world. Some of Jesus' predictions seem to point in that direction:

> And there will be signs in sun and moon and stars, and upon the earth distress of nations in perplexity at the roaring of the sea and the waves, men faint-ing with fear and with foreboding of what is coming on the world; for the powers of the heavens will be shaken (Lk. 21:25-26).

Is Jesus really speaking of the end of the world? If so, how would Jesus' advice to head for the hills and stay out of the city make any sense if the whole world were in tribulation? Saint Augustine notes that Jesus

---

[3] According to Eusebius, they fled to a town in Peraea called Pella. Eusebius, *The History of the Church from Christ to Constantine*, trans. G. A. Williamson (Middlesex, England: Dorset Press, 1984), 111.

seems to make reference "to the destruction of the earthly Jerusalem," but

> when he speaks of that destruction he generally uses language suitable to describing the end of the world and the last great day of judgment; so that the two events cannot possibly be distinguished except by comparing parallel statements on this subject in the three evangelists.[4]

The prediction of the end of the Temple and the prediction of the end of the world are indistinguishable for a reason. Jesus' first coming ushers in the judgment upon the Temple and Jerusalem; the description of their demise is a foreshadowing of the second coming of Jesus when He will judge the whole world. What happens to the Temple when it is found unfaithful is intended to be a sign of what will happen when Jesus comes back to judge the world. At the end of the Old Covenant, the master returned to settle accounts. This is not simply a history lesson but a preview of what the master will do when He comes at the end of the New Covenant. The events are so similar that they seem identical.

The Climactic Coming

The *Benedictus*, "Blessed is he who comes in the name of the Lord," marks the climactic conclusion of the travel narrative. Throughout Jesus' journey to Jerusalem, He had spoken of coming, either directly or in parables. With the triumphal procession into

---

[4] Saint Augustine, *The City of God*, trans. Henry Bettenson (New York: Penguin Books, 1984), 902.

Jerusalem the parables are unveiled. Jesus is the "Lord" who is returning from the wedding banquet, the "Lord" who comes with kingly power to judge the faithfulness of the servants. The "coming" in the parables points to the real coming of Jesus to Jerusalem. Often these parables have been taken as referring simply to Jesus' second coming, the parousia. Here it is not a matter of "either-or," but of "both-and." The stories of the Lord's coming and the subsequent judgment relate first to Jesus' climactic coming to Jerusalem and secondly to Jesus' final coming at the end of time, when the world is judged. Too often we focus on the second coming of Christ to the neglect of the first coming. In doing so, we lose proper focus of the future coming of Christ, because understanding the first is essential for grasping the import of the second.

Eucharistic Coming

There is another coming of Jesus, however, which relates to the parables and instructions of the travel narrative. In the Church's liturgy, we, like the disciples who welcomed Jesus to Jerusalem, greet Jesus with the *Benedictus*, "Blessed is he who comes in the name of the Lord." With the *Benedictus* the Church hails Jesus who will become truly present on the altar. Each and every Eucharist is a coming of Jesus. Cardinal Ratzinger has insightfully noted the correlation between Jesus' coming to Jerusalem and His continual Eucharistic coming:

> In the Old Testament text this verse [the *Benedictus*, Ps. 118:26] is a blessing at the arrival of the festive procession in the temple; on Palm Sunday

it received a new meaning which, however, had already been prepared in the development of Jewish prayer, for the expression "he who comes" had become a name for the Messiah. When the youths of Jerusalem shout this verse to Jesus, they are greeting him as the Messiah, as the king of the last days who enters the Holy City and the temple to seize possession of them. The *Sanctus* is ordered to the eternal glory of God; in contrast, the *Benedictus* refers to the advent of the incarnate God in our midst. *Christ, the one who has come, is also always the one coming. His Eucharistic coming, the anticipation of His hour, makes a present occurrence out of a promise and brings the future into the here and now.* For this reason the *Benedictus* is meaningful both as an approach to the consecration and as an acclamation to the Lord who has become present in the Eucharistic species. The great moment of His coming, the immensity of His Real Presence in the elements of the earth, definitely call for a response. The elevation, genuflection, and the ringing of the bells are such faltering attempts at a reply.[5]

Are we the servants who are ready to receive the Lord, or are we like the sleepy servants who are unprepared for the coming of the Lord? Do we realize that in receiving the Eucharist we receive the Lord, and He visits us as He did Jerusalem? Just as Jesus' coming to Jerusalem climaxed with His entry into the Temple, the Eucharistic coming of Jesus culminates with Jesus' entry into our bodies, which are temples of the Holy Spirit. We should reflect on Jesus'

---

[5] Cardinal Joseph Ratzinger, *A New Song for the Lord: Faith in Christ and Liturgy Today* (New York: Crossroad Publishing Company, 1997), 144, emphasis added.

Eucharistic coming in light of the sayings and parables in Luke's travel narrative regarding the coming of the Lord. We must receive the true presence of Jesus in the Eucharist with devotion and love. We do not want it to be said of us what Jesus sadly said of Jerusalem, that we failed to realize the time of our "visitation" (Lk. 19:44). The Eucharistic coming of Jesus prepares us for the final coming, when Jesus will return with kingly power and glory.

Coming or Going?

Jesus' arrival in Jerusalem marks the end of a long trek begun on the Mount of Transfiguration. Now that Jesus has finally come to Jerusalem, after "setting his face" with prophetic resolve, He is ready to complete His mission. According to the revelations on the Mount of Transfiguration, Jesus has come to Jerusalem in order to make His "exodus." The King's coming is brief, for He has come to Jerusalem so as to go to the Father. Now there is only one road left for Jesus to journey upon, the road to Calvary.

*   *   *

Questions for Reflection
or Group Discussion

1. (a) What are some ways in which the Transfiguration of Jesus parallels the giving of the law on Sinai? **(b)** What is the topic of conversation between Jesus,

Moses, and Elijah? **(c)** What is the significance of Jesus' shining with glory like Moses did on Sinai?

_____

_____

_____

_____

2. (a) How is Jesus' prophetic mission similar to Ezekiel's? **(b)** How do Jesus' warnings to Jerusalem parallel Ezekiel's? **(c)** Why does Jesus, on His way to Jerusalem, teach parables about a master who is coming home to check up on his stewards? **(d)** How does Jesus' prophecy about the destruction of the Temple (Lk. 21) relate to the end of the world? **(e)** How is the first coming of Jesus similar to and different from His second coming?

_____

_____

_____

_____

_____

3. (a) In what ways does Jesus' entry into Jerusalem illustrate that He is the King of Israel? **(b)** How does Jesus' journey to Jerusalem and entrance into the Temple fulfill the prophecy of Malachi?

_____

_____

_____

_____

4. (a) Why do we say or sing the *Benedictus*, "Blessed is he who comes in the name of the Lord," at Mass? **(b)** How does the *Benedictus* at Mass relate to the disciples' singing to Jesus as He entered Jerusalem on Palm Sunday? **(c)** The parables about a master's coming home relate to Jesus' coming to the Temple and to His second coming, but how do they relate to Jesus' coming in the Eucharist? **(d)** How can we read the parables about a master's coming in terms of Jesus' coming to us in the Eucharist?

_____

_____

_____

_____

7

CELEBRATING THE NEW EXODUS
—LUKE 15, 22—

Jesus' goal in journeying to Jerusalem is the inauguration of a new exodus. This was the topic of conversation between Jesus and Moses on the Mount of Transfiguration. As with the first exodus of Israel, there cannot be a new exodus without a Passover meal. And so Jesus' "coming" to Jerusalem reaches its climax "when the hour came" (Lk. 22:14) for the Passover to be celebrated.

Indeed, the celebration of the Passover is one of Jesus' main reasons for coming to Jerusalem. Jesus reveals this to His disciples at the very beginning of the Passover feast: "I have earnestly desired to eat this passover with you" (Lk. 22:15). As we shall see, this desire is for a regathering of sinners around the family banquet table of the Father. The ancient Jewish Passover feast celebrated the exodus from Egypt, but now Jesus makes this the occasion of the new redemption. This time, however, the redemption is not from Egyptian slavery but from slavery to sin. Thus, Jesus transforms the Passover into the celebration of the new exodus and the inauguration of the kingdom of God through the New Covenant.

The significance of the Passover feast is anticipated throughout Jesus' ministry by His frequent celebration at table with sinners who are returning to God through Him. Just as Jesus' own coming to Jerusalem is foreshadowed and understood in light of His stories about a master's "coming" home, so too Jesus' Last Supper Passover feast is foreshadowed and understood through His stories about banquets and His own feasting during His Galilean ministry. Indeed, the significance of Jesus' Passover cannot be fully appreciated until Jesus' table fellowship is understood. We shall therefore begin our study of Jesus' climactic Passover, from which He embarks on His exodus, with an examination of the role of table fellowship in Jesus' ministry.

Turning the Tables on Social Norms

Jesus sparked considerable controversy and opposition by the company He kept. His inclusive table fellowship was a continual source of friction with the Pharisees. Early in His ministry, Jesus encountered stiff opposition to His practice of eating with "sinners and tax collectors." When He answered an invitation from Levi, the tax collector, and attended a "great feast" in His honor, the scribes and Pharisees murmured, "Why do you eat and drink with tax collectors and sinners?" (Lk. 5:29-30). Later on, when the crowds were gathering around Jesus, they again complained, saying, "This man receives sinners and eats with them" (Lk. 15:2).

These controversies continued up to the last days of Jesus' mission when, just before entering Jerusalem, Jesus came to the house of Zacchaeus, to which the Pharisees responded by murmuring, "He has gone in to be the guest of a man who is a sinner" (Lk. 19:7). What is it about Jesus' simple act of sharing meals with sinners and tax collectors that was so scandalous to the Pharisees?

In the Mediterranean world of the first century, particularly in Israel, meals were a social event whose significance went far beyond the need to satisfy physical hunger. In a culture that had no television or radio, meals broke up the monotony of the day. It was the primary occasion for social gathering, and thus meals were laden with social stipulations. The kind of food one ate and where one sat at table were governed by social norms. The order around the table reflected the hierarchical order of society. Meals were usually eaten with one's extended family, and any invitation to dinner was a symbolic welcome into the family. Meals were a powerful token of friendship, intimacy, and trust. To betray one with whom you had shared a meal was an unspeakable crime in the ancient world. To have a meal together meant more than shared food; it gave shared identity.

In addition to such cultural customs regarding meals, the Jews themselves lived under dietary precepts that were given in the law of Moses. One of the earmarks of Jewish identity was the kosher laws, special laws governing how Jews ate and what they could eat (e.g., pork was forbidden). The Pharisees intensified the cultural significance of table fellowship and the kosher laws by demanding that the stringent food laws that governed the behavior of the Temple priests be extended to govern the eating of all foods by all of Israel. The Pharisees magnified the meaning of meals to the point that they became religious acts, like prayer and fasting. One had to sit at table with the same kind of ritual purity that a priest was required to keep when serving at the altar, thus making meals a symbolic statement of Jewish identity. Given the holiness of the meal, the Pharisees held that one could not be at table with those who were unclean; anyone not zealous in observing the Torah was excluded from their table. The Pharisees were scrupulous about what was eaten, how it was eaten, and with whom it was eaten. Meals with Gentiles and their unkosher food were prohibited.

In the eyes of the Pharisees, Jesus' presence at the table of Levi, the tax collector, was worse than bad social etiquette; it was a breach of piety. Tax collectors were despised for being treacherous accomplices to the Roman and Herodian authorities. Their inevitable contact with Gentiles made them ritually unclean and, according to the Pharisees, to eat with them would be ritually defiling. This is why the Pharisees are so scandalized by Jesus' coming to a feast hosted by, and filled with, tax collectors and sinners. How could a respectable Jew, not to mention a rabbi and prophet, break the social taboos and eat with religious outcasts? Did He not realize that to eat with such people was to give them tacit acceptance? And did He not realize that to eat with such people would make Him unclean?

Jesus responds to the Pharisees' incredulous questioning of His table fellowship with an analogy, "Those who are well have no need of a physician, but those who are sick; I have not come to call the righteous, but sinners to repentance" (Lk. 5:31-32). Jesus acknowledges that the people at this banquet are far from perfect, in fact they are "sick" with sin. But far from accepting their sinfulness, He has come as a physician for their healing. His point is implicit yet unmistakable: The policy of quarantine cannot cure the sick or free the enslaved. In fact, the old policy of quarantine is no longer needed. In the Old Testament, dietary laws were given as a means to protect Israel

from eating with pagans and falling into pagan idola-
try, much as a fence is put up to protect a child from
running into the street. But with Jesus, who is filled
with the Holy Spirit, such protections are no longer
needed. Jesus is not defiled or made unclean by eating and drinking with sinners, but rather His presence
brings about the healing and restoration of those with
whom He is feasting. Those who were once excluded
from the family feast are now restored as family
members with Jesus at the family banquet. Jesus
has not come to call the righteous, but the sinners
to repentance. This point should make the Pharisees
think twice when Jesus later accepts their invitation
to dinner.

Prodigal Son

Luke's travel narrative could almost be called the
feasting narrative, because so much of Jesus' teaching is given in the context of a meal or uses a meal as
an illustration. An example of this occurs in Lk. 15,
where Jesus, while at a feast, is teaching a crowd of
tax collectors and sinners. The Pharisees, feeling that
Jesus is once again undermining Jewish identity
and popular piety, are scandalized. Jesus responds
by telling three parables, or stories, that explain His
practice of eating with notorious sinners. Each story
climaxes with a celebration not too different from the
one that has provoked the scandal.

The first two stories are short and quite similar.
In the first a shepherd who loses a sheep leaves the
ninety-nine to seek out the one which is lost. Finding
it, the shepherd calls together his friends and neighbors, saying, "Rejoice with me, for I have found my

sheep which was lost" (Lk. 15:6). The second story concerns a woman who lost a silver coin. After a diligent search, she finds the coin and calls together her friends and neighbors. She repeats the now-familiar refrain, "Rejoice with me, for I have found the coin which I had lost" (Lk. 15:9). In each case there is rejoicing and celebration when the lost is found. These brief stories set up the climactic parable, the story of the prodigal son.

Although the story is a familiar and favorite one, often its retelling is done apart from its larger context in the fifteenth chapter of Luke's Gospel. It must be remembered that Jesus is telling the story of the prodigal son as an explanation for His own feasting with sinners. The story begins with a man and his two sons. The younger of the sons comes to his father, requesting his share of the inheritance. Even Jesus' audience of "tax collectors and sinners" would be stunned by such a bold request. In their culture, to ask a father for one's share of the inheritance was to say, "Dad, why don't you just die and let me get on with my life with the share of inheritance that is coming to me?" The audacity of the son! How does the father react? Dying to himself and his property, he acts as if he were dead and gives his younger son his share of the inheritance. Not many days later, the younger son took his share of the family property, sold it, took the money, and left town. Again, Jesus' audience is aghast. Selling one's family land in agrarian Israel was no light matter; it marked a betrayal or foolishness of immense proportions.

The prodigal son then journeys to "a far country" (Lk. 15:13). In Jewish terms, to be in a far country was synonymous with exile. For the Jews, only the Promised Land, the Holy Land, was to be the home for God's people. The Promised Land was the great blessing promised to Abraham, and to live outside of the Promised Land was considered the worst of curses (cf. Deut. 28:63). To all ears, Jesus' story was now a story about sin and exile, a story familiar enough to every Jew. The prodigal son could not sink lower, and yet he does. Famine strikes and the prodigal is destitute and hungry. Taking whatever work he can find, the prodigal eventually gets a job feeding swine. Surely this would bring a gasp or two from the crowd, for a pig is seen as the most unclean animal to the Jews. The prodigal has defiled himself by his service to pagans, and made himself unclean by his contact with prostitutes and swine. The prodigal's plight has brought him to the depths of exile and shame. But a deep conversion occurs—the prodigal comes to his senses and resolves,

> I will arise and go to my father, and I will say to him, "Father, I have sinned against heaven and before you; I am no longer worthy to be called your son; treat me as one of your hired servants" (Lk. 15:18-19).

Now there is a radical reversal in the story. By leaving home and taking his share of the inheritance, the son acted as though his father were dead. Now, the son decides to act as if he were dead, by intending to ask that his father treat him as just another hired hand. "And he arose and came to his father" (Lk. 15:20). Notice that Jesus says the prodigal "arose" and returned to his father. The word here for "arose" is the same word used later to describe Jesus' Resurrection. The significance is clear: Repentance and returning to the Father lead to a "resurrection."

While the son was on his way home, the father sees him from a distance, "had compassion and ran and embraced him and kissed him" (Lk. 15:20). The prodigal is given the welcome not of a servant, but of a son. The father's acceptance of his wayward son is unexpected. He gives his son a kiss, the sign of sha-lom or peace, even before the prodigal can speak his words of repentance. The father gives his son further tokens of acceptance, welcoming him home with the best robe, a ring, and sandals. And, as in the climaxes of the two preceding parables, the father calls for the fatted calf and says, "[L]et us eat and make merry; for this my son was dead, and is alive again; he was lost, and is found" (Lk. 15:23-24). Just as in the other two parables, there is a celebration in honor of the lost being found.

Given the context of the story, the point of the parable comes into stark focus. Jesus' table fellow-ship with sinners and tax collectors is a celebration of the lost being found, the spiritually dead being resurrected. The return of the lost is celebrated, not only on earth, but also in heaven. Jesus makes this clear when He says, "I tell you, there will be more joy in heaven over one sinner who repents than over ninety-nine righteous persons who need no repen-tance" (Lk. 15:7). Jesus is, as it were, saying to the Pharisees, "I am feasting with sinners to celebrate their return to the Father!" Jesus is playing the role of the Father, accepting the prodigal sons back into the family, the People of God. Those who were once slaves to sin are welcomed back, like the prodigal son, into the Family of God.

What is the Pharisees' response? That is the final point of the parable. As the older son comes home from the field, he hears the celebration and calls a servant to find out what is going on. The servant tells him the story of his younger brother's return and reconciliation with the father. "But he was angry and refused to go in. His father came out and entreated him" (Lk. 15:28). Notice that the older son, symbolically, refuses to go "in" while the father comes "out" to where he is, hoping to bring him inside, home, with the younger son. "It was fitting to make merry and be glad, for this your brother was dead, and is alive; he was lost, and is found" (Lk. 15:32).

The father's words to the older son are intended by Jesus to address the Pharisees who stand outside the banquet murmuring. Jesus tells the story of the prodigal son in the hope that the Pharisees will come in and join the celebration. The story functions both as an explanation of Jesus' table fellowship, and as an invitation to the Pharisees to join Jesus and the prodigals at the family table. Thus the last lines of the parable question the Pharisees' own questioning of Jesus' table fellowship.

Jesus ends the story there with the father's invitation, not telling us what the response of the older son is. This is intentional, for Jesus is leaving the door open to the Pharisees. Like the prodigal's father, Jesus invites them to come in and celebrate with Him the return of the lost.

Wedding Feast

Feasting with sinners was such a characteristic aspect of Jesus' ministry that some asked why He and His disciples did not fast like the disciples of John the Baptist and the Pharisees. Jesus answered with a question, "Can you make wedding guests fast while the bridegroom is with them?" (Lk. 5:34). The point was simple. According to custom, the Pharisees fasted twice a week, but an exception was made for those invited to a wedding. A Jewish wedding was celebrated by a week-long feast, during which one was exempt from fasting. Jesus' presence, like that of a bridegroom at a wedding feast, calls for celebration. As long as Jesus is with the disciples, they are exempt from fasting because it is a time for rejoicing and celebration.

The prophet Isaiah had foretold that the time of Israel's redemption would be marked by rejoicing and gladness (Is. 25:9). The salvation of Israel was to be celebrated by Yahweh and the people with a great feast (Is. 25:6). There is good evidence that the Jews of Jesus' day eagerly anticipated the long-awaited messianic feast that would mark the redemption of Israel. In fact, Luke records dialogue on this expectation in his Gospel. One time when Jesus was at table, someone declared to Him how blessed those were who would be present at the messianic banquet: "Blessed is he who shall eat bread in the kingdom of God!" (Lk. 14:15). Jesus Himself spoke of the messianic feast when asked about salvation: "And men will come from east and west, and from north and south and *sit at table in the kingdom of God*" (Lk. 13:29). When the kingdom of God came, it would be celebrated by sit-ting at table. Feasting is central to Jesus' teaching and ministry, because He is the Messiah who brings about the long-awaited redemption and messianic feast.

Timing Is Everything

As Jesus makes His way to Jerusalem, telling stories about the coming of a master and His banquet, He is setting the scene for His celebration of the feast of Passover. The twin themes of His travel narrative, "coming" and "feasting," merge with His arrival at Jerusalem at the time of the Passover. Jesus has carefully timed His coming to the Holy City to occur at the moment of the great Jewish feast of Passover. Why Passover? In accordance with the pattern of the prophets, Jesus chose to perform all His important actions at highly symbolic times. Jesus could have come at any time to the Temple and Jerusalem. He could have allowed Himself to be arrested and put to death much earlier (e.g., Nazareth). Undoubtedly, Jesus purposefully chose Passover as the time for His messianic meal, the Last Supper, and for His Passion and death. The aim of Jesus' mission was closely bound to the meaning of the Passover, and so He associates the culmination of His ministry and mission with the great paschal feast.

Since Jesus intended the significance of His Last Supper and Passion to be interpreted in the context of Passover, it is necessary to briefly examine the symbolism of the Passover celebration for the Jews of Jesus' day. The feast of Passover commemorated the ancient exodus of the Israelites from the bondage of Egypt. The feast celebrated the liberation of Israel from her enemies and her freedom from the shackles of slavery. To the Jews of Jesus' day, the feast of Passover evoked the imagery of liberation, a liberation that gave birth to a nation, in much the same way as the Fourth of July does for Americans. At Passover, every Jewish family ate bitter herbs as part of their Passover meal to remind them of Israel's bitter experience of slavery in Egypt. The Jews of Jesus' day would not only think of the past when celebrating this feast; they would also see the Passover as a sign of future liberation. The Passover would evoke Isaiah's prophecy that there would be a new exodus even greater than the exodus from Egypt (Is. 52). This prophecy may have been the source for the Jewish tradition that the future redemption of Israel would come on the night of the Passover.[1]

In the time of Jesus, the identity of the Passover with liberation was highlighted by Pilate's custom of freeing one Jewish prisoner at the time of the Passover (cf. Mk. 15:6; Lk. 23:15-25). The liberation of a prisoner may have been seen by the Jews as a sign of the future liberation of all Israel from Rome. Assuredly the Jews cherished the hope of another exodus amidst the chastisement of pagan occupation.

The Passover

The connotations of liberation and redemption that the Passover evoked could only have intensified as the apostles went to prepare the Passover for the man they knew to be the Messiah. Preparations must have been made with anxious anticipation. Whereas

---

[1] See *Mekilta Exodus* 12:42; see also R. H. Stein, "The Last Supper," in *Dictionary of Jesus and the Gospels*, eds. Joel B. Green, Scot McKnight, I. Howard Marshall (Downers Grove, IL: InterVarsity Press, 1992), 449.

their custom was to dine and stay in Bethany (just outside Jerusalem), Jesus sent Peter and John to prepare the Passover in the city, which followed the Jewish regulation that the Passover be celebrated within the city limits of Jerusalem. Usually meals were eaten in the late afternoon, but the Passover meal was eaten in the evening, to reenact the time of the original Passover meal (Ex. 12:6). Thus the phrase "when the hour came" (Lk. 22:14) refers to the evening time that marked the Passover. The burning question in the minds of the apostles must have been: "Is this going to be *the* Passover that will inaugurate the new exodus, the redemption of Israel?" The immensity of the moment was also felt by Jesus, who also anticipated this feast: "I have earnestly desired to eat this passover with you before I suffer" (Lk. 22:15). These words disclose that this Passover had special significance to Jesus, and that it was closely associated in Jesus' mind with His suffering.

The entire Passover celebration was designed to relive the exodus event. The host of the Passover was to direct the meal, during which he would retell the story of the exodus (Ex. 12:26-27). The Passover supper is structured by the taking of four cups of wine mixed with water, and the host interprets the symbolic supper by relating it to the exodus. Jesus, who takes the cup and speaks, is clearly the host. The bread and wine fit the Passover meal, but it is Jesus' interpretation, the words that make explicit the meaning of the meal, which puts new wine, so to speak, in the old Passover wineskins.

Jesus takes the bread, breaks it, and says, "This is my body which is given for you" (Lk. 22:19). The act of breaking the bread is a prophetic sign that symbolizes the imminent breaking of Jesus' body on the Cross. Jesus then takes the cup and says, "This cup which is poured out for you is the new covenant in my blood" (Lk. 22:20). Jesus identifies the contents of the cup with His blood. Just as with the breaking of the bread, the cup which is "poured out" prophetically signifies the shedding of His blood on the Cross. In the context of the Passover, the bloody sacrifice was supposed to be a lamb. Luke reminds us of this at the outset of his Passover narrative, stating that on that day "the passover lamb had to be sacrificed" (Lk. 22:7). In the story of the first exodus, it is the blood of the lamb that saves: "The blood shall be a sign for you . . . and when I see the blood, I will pass over you" (Ex. 12:13).

At the Last Supper there is bread and wine, but no mention of a lamb, the key element of the Passover. The absence of a lamb is deliberate. Jesus is the lamb, and now it is His blood that saves. The blood of Jesus is later identified with the Passover lamb by Peter in his first epistle: "You know that you were ransomed . . . with the *precious blood* of Christ, like that of a lamb without blemish or spot" (1 Pet. 1:18-19). And Saint Paul would later refer to Christ as "our paschal lamb" (1 Cor. 5:7).

In the first Passover in Egypt, it was not enough simply to sacrifice the lamb; the lamb also had to be eaten. "They shall eat the flesh [of the lamb] that night, roasted; with unleavened bread and bitter herbs they shall eat it" (Ex. 12:8). Therefore the Passover meal was an essential part of the sacrifice; the eating of the meal not only celebrated redemption, it helped to bring it about! Jesus, as prophetically foretold in the breaking of the bread and the pouring out of the wine, will die a sacrificial death on the Cross. And just like the Passover lamb, not only must the lamb be sacrificed, it must be eaten as well. Thus Jesus gives us His body and blood so that we can share in His atoning death and in His divine life.

The significance of Jesus' reference to a "new covenant in my blood" could not be overstated. Blood was an essential element in covenants. Ancient covenants had to be sealed with blood, which was shared between the two parties to signify their new kinship relationship. Since blood constituted kinship, its sharing signified the extension of family ties. This is seen especially at the climax of the exodus, when Israel made her national covenant with Yahweh at Sinai. There Moses took the blood of the sacrifices and poured out half upon the altar for Yahweh, and half upon the people. Thus Israel and Yahweh were now united as one family.

It was common practice among pagans to consume the blood of sacrificed animals, so as to share in the animals' "life force." According to Jewish law, certain animals could be sacrificed but their blood was never to be drunk: "You shall not eat the blood of any creature, for the life of every creature is its blood; whoever eats it shall be cut off" (Lev. 17:14). Life was identified with blood; to partake of an animal's blood was to share in its life. Eating the meat of sacrificial animals was allowed, because that signified sharing in the animal's death, a dying to animal nature.

Jesus' giving of His own blood for the disciples to drink seemed to fly in the face of Jewish practice. How could Jesus offer His blood to be drunk? Whereas partaking in the blood of animals was demeaning, partaking of the blood of Jesus was to share in the life of the God-man, to be elevated to share in the divine nature. God did not want man to sink to the level of the beasts, but rather He "earnestly desired" (Lk. 22:15) that men "become partakers of the divine nature" (2 Pet. 1:4). In previous covenants, animals were sacrificed and their blood poured out as a token sign of shared kinship, but Jesus goes beyond this in giving a sign (sacrament) that effects reality. He actually gives us a share in His blood so that we can truly become children of God. This is why the early Christians called each other brethren, for they saw themselves as members of the Family of God.

Jesus' discussion of blood in the context of the Passover meal also recalls the covenant made at the climax of the first exodus, the covenant mediated by Moses at Sinai. Jesus, however, does not simply recall the covenant; He reconstitutes it. For a Jew to speak of a "new" covenant would be as radical as for an American to speak of a "new" constitution. Not only did the adjective "new" imply a fundamental change in the covenant constitution of Israel, it evoked a powder keg-like prophecy. The prophet Jeremiah, in one of the boldest prophecies of the Old Testament, claimed that God would make a new covenant with Israel, and that this new covenant would come about when Israel was redeemed from exile and pardoned from all her sin:

> Behold, the days are coming, says the LORD, when
> I will make a *new covenant* with the house of Israel

and the house of Judah, not like the covenant which I made with their fathers when I took them by the hand to bring them out of the land of Egypt, my covenant which they broke, though I was their husband, says the LORD (Jer. 31:31-32).

Jesus had taken hold of this hope to turn the tide of history. This Passover meal was not going to be just another remembrance of the past exodus and covenant; it was to usher in the new exodus and seal the new covenant redemption of Israel.

Jesus transforms the Passover into the event of the new exodus. His blood marks the new Passover and brings salvation, not from slavery to Egypt, but from slavery to sin. The first exodus marked the great event of salvation that climaxed with the sealing of the old covenant. At that time, Yahweh commanded that the Passover be celebrated annually in order to recall Israel's salvation (Ex. 12:14, 17). Likewise, Jesus tells the disciples, "Do this in remembrance of me" (Lk. 22:19). Since redemption comes through Jesus, all remembrance is to point back to His Passover, which brings salvation to the world.

The breaking of His body and the outpouring of His blood on the Cross are the sacrifice of the definitive Passover lamb. The purpose behind the pouring out of Jesus' blood is twofold. First, His blood stands for the Passover lamb, which is a sacrifice that atones for sins and brings about redemption. Second, Jesus' blood seals the New Covenant. So the precious blood of Christ washes away our identity as sinners in order to grant us the New Covenant identity as sons and daughters of the Father, blood-brethren with Christ. We are saved from sin for sonship.

Do This in Memory of Me

Jesus made table fellowship a central aspect of His ministry. He welcomed sinners and sat down at table with them to celebrate their return. All these celebrations anticipated His Last Supper. In His deeds, parables, and teachings, Jesus spoke about table fellowship in the kingdom of God. The royal table is the table of the Father, who invites His prodigal children to return home. While at the Passover meal, Jesus said that He would not eat and drink "until it is fulfilled in the kingdom of God" (Lk. 22:16). The ultimate banquet, which according to Jesus' parables is to take place when the master comes home from the wedding banquet, is the final and glorious banquet in heaven, of which the Eucharist—Jesus' Passover—is but a foretaste. In the divine liturgy of the Church (in a text used for the Byzantine paschal liturgy), one of the prayers proclaims Jesus' Passover as the great wedding banquet, thus tying together Jesus' parables about the wedding feast and His Last Supper:

> O divine Passover, to us you have spiritually united the God whom the heavens cannot contain. By you, the great wedding-chamber has been filled; all wear the wedding garment, nor is anyone thrown out for not having a wedding garment.[2]

The seer of Revelation, granted a glimpse of this heavenly banquet, described it in terms of a great wedding feast, which fits well with Jesus' stories of a

---

[2] As quoted by Raniero Cantalamessa in *The Mystery of Easter* (Collegeville, MN: Liturgical Press, 1993), 79.

"great banquet" and "wedding feast." And upon seeing the end time, or eschatological feast, an angel says to him, "Write this: Blessed are those who are invited to the marriage supper of the Lamb" (Rev. 19:9). Will we answer the invitation to rise and dine with the Lamb?

One of Jesus' parables is all about an invitation to a "great banquet" (Lk. 14:16-24). When the invitations are rejected, the master sends out his servants to gather "the poor and maimed and blind and lame" (Lk. 14:21), a grouping that seems to describe those whom Isaiah foretold would receive the good news (cf. Is. 61:1; Lk. 4:18). As for those originally invited, the master declares, "For I tell you, none of those men who were invited shall taste my banquet" (Lk. 14:24). Immediately following this parable, Jesus summons His audience to make a commitment to follow Him as disciples. And right after that, significantly enough, Jesus is at table, inviting the Pharisees to join Him by telling the story of the prodigal son. The question from the parable is poignant: Will the crowds and the Pharisees accept Jesus' invitation to "taste and see" (Ps. 34:8) the goodness of the Lord?

This question applies to us as well. Will we come to the holy table of Mother Church and answer the summons of Jesus to "do this in remembrance of me"? (Lk. 22:19).

*   *   *

Questions for Reflection
or Group Discussion

1. (a) How does the significance of meals differ today as compared to Jesus' day? **(b)** Is it difficult for our culture of fast-food to understand the importance of meals in the Gospels?

_____

_____

_____

2. (a) Why did Jesus' table fellowship provoke such controversy? **(b)** How did Jesus explain His purpose of feasting with sinners?

_____

_____

_____

_____

3. (a) How does the larger context of Lk. 15 shed light on the parable of the prodigal son? **(b)** In what ways does the story of the prodigal son parallel the story of Israel? **(c)** In what ways does the story of the prodigal son apply to our own life stories?

_____

_____

_____

_____

_____

_____

4. (a) Why do you think Jesus "earnestly desired" to eat the Passover with His disciples? **(b)** Why did God forbid the Jews from drinking the blood of any creature, and then give us the blood of His Son to drink? **(c)** Why is blood so significant in making covenants? **(d)** What is the twofold purpose of Jesus' pouring out His blood for us?

_____

_____

_____

_____

_____

5. (a) Do Christians have a strong sense of expectation and longing for the final eschatological feast—the marriage supper of the Lamb? **(b)** If not, how can we increase our desire and hope for heaven?

_____

_____

_____

_____

_____

8

THE NEW PASCHAL LAMB
OF THE NEW EXODUS
—LUKE 23-24—

Lessons on the Road to Emmaus

The faith and hope of the disciples died with Jesus on the Cross. Despite the report from several women that Jesus' tomb was found empty, the disciples did not dare to hope and failed to find faith (cf. Lk. 24:11). Later that day, two disciples confessed, to an apparent stranger along the road to Emmaus, that they "had hoped that he [Jesus] was the one to redeem Israel" (Lk. 24:21). To the disciples, suffering and death disqualified Jesus from being the "one to redeem Israel." They failed to recognize that the stranger was actually Jesus, for His identity remained hidden so long as the meaning of the Cross remained closed to their minds. Jesus upbraided them for their foolishness, since the Scriptures had foretold that the Messiah must first suffer and then be glorified (Lk. 24:25-26). Jesus' suffering and death, far from disproving authentic messiahship, actually confirmed it. Along the road to Emmaus, Jesus opened the Scriptures and thereby unlocked the meaning of the Cross.

Jesus used Scripture to pry open the minds of the disciples to the meaning of His messianic mission. Jesus "opened their minds to understand the scriptures" (Lk. 24:45) as "he interpreted to them in all the scriptures the things concerning himself" (Lk. 24:27). Saint Paul proclaimed that Jesus' death and Resurrection in accordance with Scripture is of "first importance" in our Christian faith (1 Cor. 15:3). Both Jesus and Paul explained the Cross and empty tomb by referring to the Jewish Scriptures, the Old Testament. What, however, did Jesus and Paul mean when they announced that Jesus' Passion fulfills "all the scriptures" (Lk. 24:27; cf. 1 Cor. 15:3)?

To say that Jesus' death and Resurrection fulfills the Scriptures means more than that many scriptural texts and prophecies are accomplished in Christ. The whole is greater than the sum of its parts, and this is particularly true about the sacred Scriptures. The Bible is not just a random collection of law and prophecy, put together like some sacred encyclopedia. Rather, its primary structure is that of a story. To carve up the narrative to obtain a list of proof-texts would be to lose sight of the forest through the trees. The Bible is a narrative that tells the story of the covenant drama played out between God and His people. To say that Jesus fulfills the Scriptures is to say that in Him is the fulfillment of the biblical story. The great drama of salvation does not simply give cryptic clues to the life of Christ; it gives the very story line, or plot, of which Christ is the climax. In addition to bringing the story of Jesus to its culmination, Jesus' death and Resurrection brings the entire story of the Old Testament, from Adam to Israel, to its climactic conclusion as well. The Gospel of Luke, like the rest of the Gospels, does not simply tell the story of Jesus, but rather narrates the story of Jesus as the last and pivotal chapter of Israel's story.

In order to catch a glimpse of how Jesus' dying and rising brings the story of Scripture to its long-awaited climax, we shall reflect briefly upon the

Old Testament story of Adam and Israel. Adam begins the story with his tragic transgression, which leads to his expulsion from the Garden of Eden. Adam's exile from Eden is recapitulated, that is repeated, in Israel's life. Israel takes possession of the new Eden, the Promised Land, and, because of her transgression of the covenant, ends up in exile.

The story of Adam and Israel is the story of exile in search of an exodus. Jesus' whole mission is focused on bringing about a new exodus from the age-old cycle of exile. Jesus accomplishes this exodus, hinted at throughout His ministry, by His death and Resurrection. Through the Passion, as we shall see, Jesus ends the exile. Jesus does this by taking on the curses that lie upon Adam and Israel for their unfaithfulness and sin. Viewing Jesus' Passion through the lens of Israel and Adam's exilic curses will bring the covenant logic of the Cross into sharp focus. This focus will help us understand—from a biblical perspective—why Jesus had to die, or as Jesus put it, why it was "necessary that the Christ should suffer these things and enter into his glory" (Lk. 24:26).

Jesus and the Story of Israel

After having Jesus arrested and interrogated, the chief priests and scribes brought Jesus to Pontius Pilate, the Roman governor of Jerusalem and Judea. They told Pilate that Jesus was an insurrectionist who was stirring up the people to rebellion against Caesar: "We found this man perverting our nation, and forbidding us to give tribute to Caesar, and saying that he himself is Christ a king" (Lk. 23:2). The charges, such as the accusation that Jesus had forbidden the paying of taxes to Caesar, were undeniably false. Far from preaching political revolution, Jesus had constantly opposed it. Jesus was innocent of insurrection. His accusers were the ones seeking a rebellion against Rome (which broke out in 66 A.D.).

This irony was not lost upon Jesus, who made some cryptic comments about it shortly after He was falsely sentenced. As Jesus was being led to the place of execution, a group of women bewailed and lamented His suffering. Jesus responded:

> Daughters of Jerusalem, do not weep for me, but weep for yourselves and for your children. For behold, the days are coming when they will say . . . to the mountains, "Fall on us"; and to the hills, "Cover us." For if they do this when the wood is green, what will happen when it is dry? (Lk. 23:28-31).

The contrast between green and dry wood is a metaphor comparing the present treatment of Jesus, who is innocent of insurrection, to the present generation's children, who will be guilty of rebellion. Jesus warns that if this is how they treat those who are innocent, imagine how horrifically they will deal with the guilty. Once again, Jesus is giving prophetic warning of the upcoming tribulation that will occur when Israel openly revolts against Rome.[1]

Jesus is charged with rebellion, but the real rebel is Israel. Jesus' condemnation as a criminal guilty of

---

[1] When Jesus says, "the days are coming," He is employing an idiom used by many of the prophets to describe a moment of judgment and punishment from the Lord. (e.g., Amos 5:18; 8:11; Joel 1:15; 2:1, 11, 31; Mal. 4:1, 5).

rebellion and Israel's condemnation for rebellion by the prophet Isaiah presents a striking parallel. The word of the Lord to Isaiah begins with God's accusation that Israel is rebellious: "Hear, O heavens, and give ear, O earth; for the Lord has spoken: 'Sons have I reared and brought up, but they have rebelled against me'" (Is. 1:2). Then the Lord upbraids Israel for continual rebelliousness, stating that such defiance will only make them suffer:

> Why will you still be smitten, that you continue to rebel? The whole head is sick, and the whole heart faint. From the sole of the foot even to the head, there is no soundness in it, but bruises and sores and bleeding wounds; they are not pressed out, or bound up, or softened with oil (Is. 1:5-6).

The corporate body of Israel is afflicted from head to foot for her rebellion. The brief description of Israel's collective suffering parallels Isaiah's later description of the affliction that the suffering servant unjustly undergoes (Is. 53). Isaiah charges Israel with rebellion and warns of her painful punishment which, surprisingly, is later inflicted upon the Lord's suffering servant, rather than the nation of Israel.

The prophetic purpose of the charges against Jesus is now evident. Jesus takes upon Himself the charge of rebellion, of which Israel was actually guilty. In doing this, Jesus becomes the suffering servant Isaiah had foreseen, the one who would be smitten from head to toe. Jesus is punished in Israel's place. Thus through the centuries Christians have seen the affliction of the suffering servant and of corporate Israel in Isaiah as prophetic descriptions of Jesus' suffering.

As Pilate is considering whether he will condemn Jesus without any evidence of wrongdoing, a large mob excitedly assembles before him. The crowd cries out, "Away with this man, and release to us Barabbas" (Lk. 23:18). Now Pilate had a custom of releasing one Jewish prisoner, each year, at the time of the Passover.[2] The people demand that Pilate release Barabbas, "a man who had been thrown into prison for an insurrection started in the city, and for murder" (Lk. 23:19). The irony is clear: Jesus is innocent of insurrection, while Barabbas is guilty. Yet they seek the death of Jesus and the release of Barabbas. The restless crowd, on the edge of riot, shouts at Pilate, "Crucify, crucify him!" (Lk. 23:21). And again Pilate confesses Jesus' innocence, saying, "Why, what evil has he done? I have found in him no crime deserving death" (Lk. 23:22). This is the fourth time in Luke's narrative that Pilate has declared Jesus guiltless. Clearly Luke wishes to highlight Jesus' innocence.

The choice between Barabbas and Jesus is larger than simply the choice between which individual will go free, and which will be executed. Israel is at a crossroads: There are two different paths before her, two ways of being Israel. Barabbas, an insurrectionist and murderer, represents the way of violent revolution. Barabbas embodies the common belief that the kingdom will come with the violent and vengeful overthrow of the Romans. Here the call is to take up the sword and rally against the Romans.

---

[2] "Now at the feast he used to release for them one prisoner whom they asked" (Mk. 15:6).

Jesus embodies and offers an altogether different approach. His way is forgiveness and peace. The kingdom will come not through the overthrow of Caesar, but of Satan. Sin, not Roman soldiers, needs to be defeated. Jesus' call is to take up one's cross and follow the Prince of Peace.

Jesus knows that the path of violent revolution, the path of Barabbas, is a dead end. Earlier that week He had cried out to Jerusalem: "Would that even today you knew the things that make for peace! But now they are hid from your eyes" (Lk. 19:42). In rejecting Jesus, the people have rejected the path to peace. By choosing Barabbas they have embraced violent revolution, and it will lead to the disastrous revolt against Rome in 66-70 A.D., which would end in the destruction of Jerusalem.

The crowd's cries for Jesus' crucifixion intensifies until Pilate's resolve melts, and he capitulates to their demands. "He released the man who had been thrown into prison for insurrection and murder, whom they asked for; but Jesus he delivered up to their will" (Lk. 23:25). Luke repeats the fact that Barabbas is an insurrectionist and murderer, underscoring the irony that the one guilty of rebellion is released whereas the one who preached against sedition is sentenced for it. Jesus takes the place of Barabbas, the innocent for the guilty. In the larger picture, Jesus takes the place not only of Barabbas, but also of all Israel. It is worth noting that the name "Barabbas" means "son of the father," and it is Israel who in the Old Testament is considered God's son, as seen in Isaiah's oracle where God declared, "Sons have I reared . . . but they have rebelled against me" (Is. 1:2). Barabbas represents the rebellious sons of God, and ultimately not just Israel, but all sinners, who make the ultimate act of rebellion, that against God the Father.

The Suffering Servant

In His Passion, Jesus fulfills the role of Isaiah's suffering servant. He becomes the scapegoat who takes upon Himself the sins of Israel. When Jesus was at table with His disciples the evening before His crucifixion, He predicted that a prophecy of Isaiah would soon be fulfilled: "For I tell you that this scripture must be fulfilled in me, 'And he was reckoned with transgressors'" (Lk. 22:37; cf. Is. 53:12). This prophecy of Isaiah comes to pass when the soldiers bring Jesus to the place called "The Skull," where they crucify Him along with two criminals, one on the right and one on the left. The prophecy from Isaiah is just one line of what is now known as the fourth servant song (Is. 52:13-53:12).

By citing this prophecy from Isaiah, Jesus identifies Himself as the suffering servant foretold by Isaiah. Not only does the single verse explicitly cited by Jesus, "he was reckoned with transgressors" (Is. 53:12), apply to Jesus, but the whole prophecy concerning the suffering servant relates to Jesus. According to Isaiah, the suffering servant was chosen by the Lord to be the scapegoat for sinners:

> Surely he has borne our griefs and carried our sorrows; yet we esteemed him stricken, smitten by God, and afflicted. But he was wounded for our transgressions, he was bruised for our iniquities; upon him was the chastisement that made us whole, and with his stripes we are healed. All we like sheep

have gone astray; we have turned every one to his own way; and the LORD has laid on him the iniquity of us all (Is. 53:4-6).

This prophecy is the key to unlocking the mystery of Jesus' unjust death. The prophecy, from the fourth servant song, comes in the context of Isaiah's predictions about a new exodus. In Is. 52, the Lord speaks of the first exodus from Egypt and announces a new exodus that will be announced to Zion as the good news, as gospel (Is. 52:3-11). The new exodus will not be made in the haste of the old, for it will be greater (Is. 52:12). After Isaiah speaks of the new exodus, he then focuses on the new Passover lamb of the new exodus—the suffering servant. Thus the servant is described like a lamb led to slaughter (Is. 53:7). By identifying Himself as the suffering servant, Jesus is claiming to be the paschal lamb of the next exodus!

Just as the high priest would take a scapegoat once a year on the day of atonement, pronounce upon it the sins of all Israel, and then sacrifice it (Lev. 16), so too Jesus takes upon Himself the sin of Israel and its punishment. He becomes the final scapegoat. Jesus, the innocent one, suffers for the guilty. He is wounded that Israel may be healed, and He dies that Israel may live. His chastisement makes the people whole.

The Crucifixion of the King

When Jesus is nailed to the Cross, He prays, "Father, forgive them; for they know not what they do" (Lk. 23:34). His intercession for those responsible for His death fulfills yet another prediction of Isaiah about the suffering servant: "[H]e bore the sin of many, and made intercession for the transgressors" (Is. 53:12). Jesus' prayer also fulfills the law of love that He Himself had laid down: "Love your enemies, do good to those who hate you . . . pray for those who abuse you" (Lk. 6:27-28).

Jesus prays for those who abuse Him, but that does not mean the abuse stops. While Jesus is hanging on the Cross, He is mocked by the Jewish leaders: "He saved others; let him save himself, if he is the Christ of God, his Chosen One!" (Lk. 23:35). The irony is that the title "Chosen One" is a title for the suffering servant (cf. Is. 42:1), and that by "his stripes we are healed" (Is. 53:5). The leaders assert that since Jesus is on the Cross, He cannot be the Messiah; what kind of messiah dies an ignoble death on a cross? The answer, according to Isaiah, is the kind who "makes himself an offering for sin" in order that he may "bear their iniquities" and "make many to be accounted righteous" (Is. 53:10-11). The Messiah brings redemption not in spite of His suffering, but *through* it.

Jesus, as predicted in Isaiah's vision of the suffering servant, takes the place of Israel, just as He takes the place of Barabbas. In order to understand this, however, we must know in what "place" Israel stood. As mentioned earlier, Israel had already been condemned by the prophets for rebellion against God and breaking the covenant. When the prophets, like Isaiah, listed all kinds of threats and warnings of the tribulation that would befall Israel for her unfaithfulness, they were simply repeating the stipulations listed in the covenant Israel made with God through

Moses. In the covenant treaty, which is the entire Book of Deuteronomy, there is a list of blessings for covenant faithfulness and curses for unfaithfulness. The threats listed by the prophets are simply the curses that are stipulated in the covenant. Thus the prophets were simply warning that the curse clauses of the covenant were going to happen once the covenant had been violated.

The curses are listed in chapter 28 of Deuteronomy. These curses are important in understanding Israel's history, which follows the script of Deuteronomy so well that one can speak of Israel's Deuteronomic destiny. The curses describe what will befall Israel when she breaks the covenant. Disease and illness will become common, and then famine and plagues, and then war and captivity to foreigners, and, after suffering exile at the hands of the Gentiles, they shall be executed. The prophets warned Israel during the time of their kings that their sin would lead to the Deuteronomic curses and exile. Israel in fact ended up in exile because these warnings went unheeded. As the prophet Daniel clearly saw, the curses of the law had been poured out upon Israel because of her sin (cf. Dan. 9:11).

To say then that Jesus, as scapegoat, took Israel's place is to say that Jesus took upon Himself the curses that were upon Israel. Thus Saint Paul observed that "Christ redeemed us from the curse of the law, having become a curse for us" (Gal. 3:13). The pattern of the Deuteronomic curses is strikingly similar to Jesus' prophetic prediction of His Passion:

> Behold, we are going up to Jerusalem, and every-
> thing that is written of the Son of man by the proph-
> ets will be accomplished. For he will be delivered
> to the Gentiles, and will be mocked and shamefully
> treated and spit upon, they will scourge him and kill
> him, and on the third day he will rise. (Lk. 18:31).

Just as Israel was to be handed over to the Gentiles
in exile and then afflicted and finally executed, so too
Jesus' Passion follows the pattern of Deuteronomy's
curses. This is why Jesus must be handed over to
Pilate, the Gentile governor. By being turned over to
the Gentiles, Jesus experiences a symbolic exile that
precedes His execution. Jesus becomes accursed so
that Israel will be freed from the curse.

Here we come to the core question of the Cross:
Why must Jesus die in order to save Israel? The biblical answer is "the covenant." Israel and Yahweh had
made a solemn covenant, and covenants—such as
marriage—are permanent. Therefore, the oaths that
Israel swore as part of the covenant, which included
the curses, could not be taken back. God and Israel
swore that breaking the covenant would end in death.
According to the curses, Israel had to be exiled and
destroyed for her unfaithfulness—unless one of the
parties were to die (Deut. 28:15-68, especially vv.
47-48).[3] Israel's death would hardly solve the problem,
and God couldn't die—or could He? According to Saint
Paul, this is exactly what God does through Jesus. God
becomes incarnate in Jesus, who then takes upon

---

[3] See Rom. 7:1-7 for Paul's discussion of how death was necessary to
end Israel's bondage to old covenant law, in which he compares the Old
Covenant to a marriage.

Himself the curses of the covenant and dies on the Cross. Thus the Old Covenant curses are annulled on the Cross. As Saint Paul says, God has "forgiven us all our trespasses, having canceled the bond which stood against us with its legal demands; this he set aside, nailing it to the cross" (Col. 2:13-14). On the Cross the curse is conquered.

Jesus and the Story of Adam

Israel, however, was not alone in suffering under a curse. The rest of the nations were under a curse as well, a curse going all the way back to Adam, the father of all. Jesus' vicarious suffering atones not only for Israel, but also for Adam and all his progeny. Luke has subtly hinted at this from the beginning of Jesus' ministry, where he traced Jesus' genealogy all the way back to Adam, (unlike Matthew's genealogy, which only goes as far back as Abraham). By making several allusions to Adam in his account of Jesus' Passion, Luke shows how Jesus is taking on the sin and curse, not only of Israel, but of Adam and all humanity.

Jesus, like Adam before Him, is tested in a garden, the garden of Gethsemane. When Jesus is praying to the Father for strength to accept the bitter cup of suffering, He prays so intensely that "his sweat became like great drops of blood falling down upon the ground" (Lk. 22:44). As one of the curses for his original sin, Adam would labor by "the sweat of [his] face" (Gen. 3:19). Luke carefully points out how the beads of Jesus' blood fall down upon the ground, the ground which was cursed because of Adam. In fact, part of Adam's curse is that the ground would bring up thorns (Gen. 3:18), and significantly enough Jesus is crowned with thorns (cf. Mt. 27:29; Mk. 15:17). Jesus takes up the agony of Adam through the pain of His Passion.

The story of Adam includes the tragic tale of exile from Eden. This exile from paradise, which is part of the curse upon Adam, is overcome by Jesus' new exodus. Jesus' dialogue with the criminal on the cross, the "good thief," alludes to this new exodus to the new Eden. The good thief cries out from his cross in faith, "Jesus, remember me when you come in your kingly power" (Lk. 23:42). This notion of Jesus' "coming" into rule echoes the parable of the talents, in which the nobleman is to "come" back from a far country where he received his kingdom. Since Jesus told that parable on the outskirts of Jerusalem, it is possible that the "good thief" was part of Jesus' audience that day, especially since he calls Jesus by name.

Whether knowingly or not, the good thief is the first to articulate the key to the parable of the talents: Jesus is the nobleman, and the journey to the "far country" is Jesus' ascension to the Father. The reward for the faithful servants in the parable is a share in the nobleman's kingdom, as on the Cross Jesus promises the criminal, "Truly, I say to you, today you will be with me in Paradise" (Lk. 23:43). The criminal recognizes the coming of the king, and so he has a share in Christ's kingdom.

The word "paradise" is only used two other times in the New Testament. Paul uses it to describe heaven (2 Cor. 12:3), and it is used in Revelation to describe heaven as the new Garden of Eden that Jesus promises to those who persevere in faithfulness: "To him who conquers I will grant to eat of the tree of life, which is in the paradise of God" (Rev. 2:7). Jesus completes on the Cross the return from the ultimate exile, the exile from the Father. With Jesus' last breath on the Cross the exile from Eden ends, and heaven is reopened to Adam and his descendants.

The ultimate curse incurred by Adam is death: "[Y]ou are dust, and to dust you shall return" (Gen. 3:19). Jesus takes this curse upon Himself by dying on the Cross. Paradoxically, Jesus' death brings life to all of Adam's descendants. Adam had been banished from the garden and its tree of life, but now Jesus makes the wood of the Cross the new tree of life, the fruit of which is taken up in the Passover cup, the cup of His blood. For those who drink and eat of Jesus' body and blood, the fruit of the new tree of life, death is defeated and Eden opened. Jesus takes the curses upon Himself, but at a high price.

Jesus' Passion is not at all what one would expect the redemption and new exodus to look like, but it must be remembered that a lamb must be sacrificed for a Passover to be celebrated. Jesus is the lamb, and He pays the debt of sin owed by both Israel and Adam. This sets in motion the great jubilee, because Jesus' Passion and death releases both Gentile and Jew from the debt of sin, slavery to the devil, and exile from the heavenly Eden.

The Resurrection and Great Commission

The two disciples traveling to Emmaus with Jesus failed to recognize Him until supper. When Jesus took up the bread, blessed it, and then broke it, "their eyes were opened and they recognized him"

(Lk. 24:31). Earlier that day Jesus had "opened" their minds by showing the relation between Himself and the Scriptures of Israel (Lk. 24:32). Now Jesus opens their eyes in the breaking of the bread, the Eucharist. The Word written and the Word made flesh in the Eucharist are the means of "opening" the disciples up to the divine mystery of Jesus and His mission. Here, in the story of Emmaus, we have a glimpse of the Mass, the Liturgy of the Word followed by the Liturgy of the Eucharist. At Emmaus, the twin themes of Jesus' coming and feasting converge when the resurrected Christ "comes" to His disciples in the breaking of bread. And He continues to come to His disciples whenever the Church gathers together to break bread in the Eucharist.

Jesus also appears to the eleven apostles in Jerusalem. Luke highlights the concreteness of the Resurrection. Jesus declares, "See my hands and my feet, that it is I myself; handle me, and see; for a spirit has not flesh and bones as you see that I have" (Lk. 24:39). He calls them to look at His hands and feet, for they bear the telltale signs of the crucifixion; Jesus is known by the scars. "Then he opened their minds to understand the scriptures" (Lk. 24:45), after which He gives them the great commission:

> Thus it is written, that the Christ should suffer and on the third day rise from the dead, and that repentance and forgiveness [release] of sins should be preached in his name to all nations, beginning from Jerusalem (Lk. 24:46-47).

Jesus calls His disciples to proclaim the good news of His new exodus to the whole world, proclaiming the "release" of sins. "Release" (*aphesis*) is the jubilee term that Jesus had made a central part of His ministry. Now it is to be at the center of the Church's mission. The disciples are to proclaim to the scattered children of Israel and Adam that there is a way out of their exile, for in Jesus one can find release from the bondage to sin and death.

Before the disciples can begin their jubilee commission, however, they must wait in Jerusalem "until you are clothed with power from on high" (Lk. 24:49). Luke will describe this "clothing with power" in the sequel to his Gospel, the Acts of the Apostles. The story of Acts is the story of the Church, and it begins in a strikingly similar way to the story of Jesus in the Gospel. Jesus began His messianic mission, as we saw in the first chapter, with the anointing of the Holy Spirit. Clothed in the power of the Spirit, Jesus is the anointed one, the Christ (Gk.), or Messiah (Heb.).

Likewise, the Church is anointed with the Spirit at Pentecost—which occurs for the individual at Baptism and Confirmation—and thus Christ's disciples in every age can truly be called "Christian," for they literally are anointed ones. The disciples are anointed in the Spirit to continue the mission of the Messiah, to continue the work of Jesus' exodus and jubilee. Now the disciples, and all of us who have been baptized, can follow Jesus' example in making our own the words of Isaiah's jubilee prophecy:

> The Spirit of the Lord is upon me, because he has anointed me to preach good news to the poor. He has sent me to proclaim release to the captives . . . to set at liberty those who are oppressed (Lk. 4:18).

Jesus continually calls all disciples to go forth and announce to the world the good news. With the great commission, the story of Jesus becomes the story of the disciples. And now it is our story too! Jesus' last words to His disciples are aimed at all who hear the Gospel: "You are witnesses of these things" (Lk. 24:48)!

*   *   *

Questions for Reflection
or Group Discussion

1. (a) Have you ever thought about how Jesus' death and Resurrection fulfill not only individual passages and prophecies of the Old Testament, but the entire story line of Scripture? **(b)** How does seeing the big picture of Scripture add to your understanding of the Cross?

_____

_____

_____

2. (a) What is so symbolic in the choice between Jesus and Barabbas? **(b)** How do they embody two different ways of obtaining the kingdom?

_____

_____

_____

_____

3. (a) Why do you think that Isaiah has been called the "fifth gospel," given the relation of the suffering servant (e.g., the fourth servant song, Is. 52:13-53:12)

to Jesus on the Cross? **(b)** Do Isaiah's striking prophecies concerning Jesus' sacrificial death strengthen
your faith?

_____

_____

_____

_____

_____

4. In what ways does Jesus take on the curse of Israel
described in Deuteronomy 28?

_____

_____

_____

_____

5. (a) What are the three curses of Adam that Jesus
takes upon Himself in His Passion and death? **(b)**
What did the tree of life in the garden of Eden give to
those who ate of it? **(c)** What is the new tree of life?

_____

_____

_____

_____

_____

6. (a) Jesus' public mission began with His anointing
in the Holy Spirit at His baptism. What event inaugu-
rates the Church's mission in the Acts of the Apostles?
(b) How and when are we anointed with the Holy

Spirit, so that we too are "christs" or Christians—that is, anointed ones? **(c)** If we are Christians—anointed ones—what is our anointing for? Specifically, what is our mission (see Mt. 28:19-20)? **(d)** Do Christians need a stronger sense of mission? How can we increase our zeal to evangelize? What can you do to be a witness for Christ?

_____

_____

_____

_____

_____

_____

Holiness for Catholic Women in Today's World!

Courageous Love is a Bible study specifically for women who want to discover God's plan for their lives. Ideal for individual or small group study, *Courageous Love* provides practical lessons for growing in the Christian life.

"*Courageous Love* guides women through Scripture and the Catechism in an exploration of who God has called us to be. What a refreshing and thought-provoking resource for individual or group study! Highly recommended."
—**Kimberly Hahn**

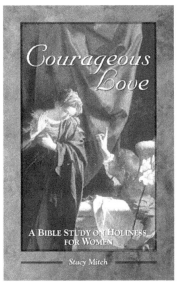

CPSIA information can be obtained
at www.ICGtesting.com
Printed in the USA
BVHW090415050122
625226BV00008B/139